COMMUNITY WORK APPROACHES TO
Child Welfare

Community Work Approaches
to Child Welfare

EDITED BY BRIAN WHARF

broadview press

NATIONAL LIBRARY OF CANADA CATALOGUING IN PUBLICATION DATA

Main entry under title:

Community work approaches to child welfare

Includes bibliographical references.
ISBN 1-55111-453-4

1. Community-based child welfare—Canada—Case studies.
2. Community-based family services—Canada—Case studies.
I. Wharf, Brian.

HV745.A6C64 2002   362.7'0971   C2001-904190-X

BROADVIEW PRESS, LTD.
is an independent, international publishing house, incorporated in 1985.

North America
Post Office Box 1243, Peterborough, Ontario, Canada K9J 7H5
3576 California Road, Orchard Park, New York, USA 14127
TEL (705) 743-8990; FAX (705) 743-8353; E-MAIL 75322.44@compuserve.com

United Kingdom and Europe
Thomas Lyster, Ltd. Unit 9, Ormskirk Industrial Park,
Old Boundary Way, Burscough Rd, Ormskirk, Lancashire L39 2YW
TEL (1695) 575112; FAX (1695) 570120; E-MAIL books@tlyster.co.uk

Australia
St. Clair Press, Post Office Box 287, Rozelle, NSW 2039
TEL (612) 818-1942; FAX (612) 418-1923

www.broadviewpress.com

Broadview Press gratefully acknowledges the financial support of the Book Publishing Industry Development Program, Ministry of Canadian Heritage, Government of Canada.

Cover Design & Typesetting
by Liz Broes, Black Eye Design.

Printed in Canada

10 9 8 7 6 5 4 3 2 1

contents

acknowledgements

My thanks goes first to the contributors to this book for their insightful case studies and for their helpful suggestions for the final chapter. I am especially grateful to Andrew Armitage, Professor, School of Social Work, University of Victoria, who, on very short notice agreed to read the manuscript and wrote a most perceptive review.

I would like also to thank Michael Harrison, vice-president of Broadview Press for first welcoming and then approving the suggestion that Broadview publish a book on community approaches to child welfare. Some years ago we worked together on a number of books and it was a delight to renew the partnership. As copy editor Richard Tallman contributed his deft touch to the manuscript.

This was the first time I have edited a book without help from secretaries and I now appreciate more than I ever did in the past the contributions made by Barbara Egan and Jean Holder. A retrospective thank you goes to both.

As always I have profited from the many suggestions made by my wife, Marilyn Callahan, who always manages to combine astute criticism with generous support. My only regret is that her many other academic pursuits prevented her from contributing a chapter or being a joint editor, an omission that I hope to rectify should I take on another publishing venture.

Introduction

BRIAN WHARF

Almost a decade ago the preface to another book on child welfare began with the following comment: "*Rethinking Child Welfare in Canada* was initiated out of a profound sense of dissatisfaction with child welfare policy and practice in this country" (Wharf, 1993). In the time that has elapsed and despite numerous efforts in all provinces to bring about improvements, the contributors to this book are of the opinion that the child welfare enterprise has steadily deteriorated. As will become clear as the discussion proceeds in the following chapters, all involved in child welfare are frustrated and deeply disappointed by the intrusiveness and sheer ineffectiveness of the enterprise. Those being served are dealt with as cases to be inspected and assessed by risk-assessment instruments and case management schemes and, not surprisingly, resent being treated as "objects." They are resentful, too, that the resources available to them severely limit their ability to care for their children. For their part, child welfare workers who enter the field to help and assist families and children are largely prevented from doing so by massive workloads and by the way in which the work is organized. Policymakers cling tenaciously to the assumption that the enterprise can be improved by increasing the control and surveillance over both staff and those being served. And these views and experiences are kept in not-so-splendid isolation since no, or at best only fragile, structures have been created to share differing realities.

Like *Rethinking Child Welfare in Canada*, this book suggests that there are ways in which child welfare can be changed and the case is argued here that community social work and community organizing are neglected but potentially powerful strategies for improving child welfare. The argument is based on case studies that describe these strategies in a number of agencies across the country and on the holistic, "community control" approach being taken in First Nation communities.

This chapter describes the objectives of the book and weaves the key concepts addressed in the book into a review of the relevant literature. The review takes on the task of unravelling the meanings attached to the familiar terms of "community development" and "community organizing" and introduces a third conceptualization of "community social work." The chapter concludes by outlining the standpoint of the contributors that while community approaches can and have made significant contributions to the well-being of children and families, their contributions can be realized most completely if nested in a set of progressive social policies. In our view building the capacity of communities complements and by no means replaces the need for national and provincial social policies.

The overall objective of the book is to analyze the attempts of child welfare agencies, which hold the legislated mandate to deal with child neglect and abuse, to incorporate community social work and community organization into their day-to-day work. Such agencies include the urban and rural offices of provincial ministries or departments, Children's Aid Societies, multi-service centres like the local community service centres (CLSCs) in Quebec and community-controlled agencies in First Nation communities. The book also includes a chapter on family resource programs that suggests there is common ground between these programs and child welfare agencies. The specific objectives are:

1. To identify the reasons why community approaches have remained on the periphery of practice.

2. To identify the ways in which community approaches could become an integral part of the mainstream approach to child welfare.

3. To describe the child welfare programs and approaches of First Nation family and child welfare agencies that have assumed control of child welfare.

What Is Community Organizing?

The literature in community development and community organizing is replete with efforts to define both terminology and strategies of action. The earliest and still one of the most useful is a framework that distinguishes between four strategies: locality development, social planning, social action, and social reform (Rothman,1974). These strategies differ from one another on a number of dimensions and particularly with regard to who holds power and in whose interests power is exercised. Locality development is based in a relatively benign view of power. It assumes that residents of a neighbourhood can come together, identify issues, and resolve these in a consensual fashion. While Rothman coined the term "locality development," the strategy has much in common with community organizing as conceived much earlier by Ross (1955) and with the more recent approach of building the capacity of communities articulated by McKnight (1995).

Social planning assumes that power is essentially benign, and emphasizes the contribution of professional planners to bring about needed changes. The converse is true of social action. Theorists and practitioners of social action believe that power is divided in a most unequal fashion: a few, the influential élite, wield a great deal of power in the political and economic affairs of the nation, while the power of the majority is largely restricted to voting in elections. Despite the fact that he died many years ago, Saul Alinsky remains the best-known practitioner of social action. Alinsky favoured two basic strategies: one designed to embarrass and the other designed to threaten individuals holding power (Alinsky, 1972).

The fourth approach, social reform, has received little attention in comparison to the three noted above. Yet, as a composite of social planning and social action, social reform accurately describes many attempts made by community groups to bring about change in matters such as housing conditions and the adequacy of social assistance rates.

The Rothman framework has been criticized by authors who argue all of the approaches take on a different hue and have different objectives depending upon the vitally important considerations of race, class, and gender. (See, among other critics, Dominelli, 1989.) A second line of criticism maintains that distinguishing between approaches "tends to create practice enclaves" (OBrien,1979: 234) rather than emphasizing their common elements. Indeed, another influential framework eschews discrimination in favour of promoting commonalities: all approaches have two essential components, "strengthening social provisions or resources and improving people's problem solving capacities and relationships" (Perlman and Gurin, 1972: 58).

Other theorists have argued that organizing is the key to bringing about understanding that will change communities (Miller, Rein, and Levitt, 1990). Some of the examples noted in this framework include organizing at a grassroots or locality level; organizing based on the identities of race, class, and gender; organizing to address issues of consumption and the environment; and organizing to achieve the objectives of mutual aid and self-help.

Community development is another term often used to describe efforts to bring about change at the community level and is the title of one of the most influential journals in the field: *Community Development, an International Forum*. Community development began with the efforts of pioneers like T.R. Batten (1957) to develop communities in developing countries, and has much in common with the capacity-building emphasis of locality development. Indeed, Batten and his colleagues were committed to a style of work that was non-directive. Nevertheless, for First Nations people community development has conjured up "images of outsiders coming into a community and voyeuristically engaging in some form of community manipulation" (Absolon and Herbert, 1997: 206).

As noted above, a recent and influential theorist is John McKnight (1995), who is critical of professionals, including community workers, who in his view have usurped the natural helping capacity of ordinary people. McKnight argues strenuously that communities have an innate capacity to care for residents and that this ability should be nourished and supported by the state, by corporations, and by charitable organizations like the United Way. His work has caught the attention of both neo-conservative politicians, who wish to dismantle the social programs of the state, and of social democrats, who are committed to enhancing the ability of citizens to participate in civic activities at a variety of levels.

Feminist writers have criticized all of the above approaches for failing to take into account the particular contribution of women. It is evident that the vast majority of the writers noted above are men, while women perform most of the day-to-day activities in communities. Callahan (1997: 183) puts the point neatly when she says that:

> What distinguishes feminist community organizing from other approaches is its insistence that all activities must be informed by an analysis of gender (and race and class) and modified on the basis of this analysis. It is also characterized by its commitment to a social movement and by its attempts to connect local level efforts to those taking place in other jurisdictions and at other levels. It differs from feminist organizing in general because of its concern with place,

with helping women in a geo-political space define their needs and aspirations and begin to work on these.

I would be remiss to conclude this discussion of approaches without mentioning the important contributions of developing-country organizers such as Paolo Freire and Gustav Gutierrez. Their work is anchored in the belief that "we shall not have our great leap forward ... until the marginalized and exploited become the artisans of their own liberation, until their voice makes itself heard directly, without mediation, without interpreters" (Gutierrez, 1983: 65). Freire and Gutierrez have articulated a process of change known as "conscientization" in which professionals provide information and support but leave the fundamental decisions in bringing about change to the oppressed. First Nations people in Canada have drawn substantially and benefited greatly from the work of these theorists. (Absolom and Herbert, 1997).

The notion of community social work is based on the "patch" or "neighbourhood" approach to providing social services in England. Writers including Smale, Adams, and Nelson (Smale, 1995; Adams and Nelson, 1995) argue convincingly that the profession of social work should discontinue its reliance on individual approaches that view those being served as clients. Adams and Nelson (1995: 103) depict the role of community social workers thus:

> Workers no longer take sole responsibility for the problem at hand. They recognize that most of the caring and monitoring is done informally in the family and neighborhood and work to build the caring capacity of the people and networks involved. Using their time to build partnerships with families and their networks, with agencies, schools, churches and neighborhood groups they help interweave formal and informal caring. They spend less time doing to or for families and more time working with them, less time on crisis intervention and more on prevention and early identification.

A number of important insights can be gleaned from the literature on community social work. While these insights may not have originated in or be unique to this literature, writers such as those noted above give explicit and careful attention to them. First, people initially look for help from friends and neighbours rather than from professionals. Second, communities besieged by such issues as poverty, inadequate housing, and high rates of crime frequently have the fewest resources and strength to deal with problems. While all communities require the backing of strong social policies, resource-poor communities require particular attention and support from senior levels of government. Third, communities should not be seen only or even primarily as convenient repositories of resources like foster homes or respite-care facilities to be used when needed by professionals. Rather, communities are networks of relationships that require constant nourishing and all residents, including those needing assistance, can contribute to the nourishing.

Community social work has much in common with community organization. There is agreement that office-based practice with individual clients who are diagnosed by experts as requiring professional help is not effective practice. There is agreement that effective practice must be based in communities rather than in large, rule-bound organizations. There is agreement that effective practice requires a philosophy of service that sees those requiring service as citizens who bring information and skills to resolving the task at hand. But community social work is essentially concerned with individuals, families, and groups and does not as a major and continuing concern address environmental and policy issues that impact negatively on residents of some neighbourhoods. "Community social work" accurately describes the case studies contained in Chapters 3 and 6, "community organizing" captures the work of the case studies in Chapter 4, and Chapter 5 is devoted to two examples of "community control."

While this book is concerned with changing practice in the field of child welfare, the community social work approach seeks to transform not just one field of service, but the social work profession. It represents a "paradigm shift which will come about when new information is introduced that cannot be accommodated in the conventional wisdom. This information will come from the voices of service users, caregivers and other significant participants in problematic social situations that will transform the way that we think about practice" (Smale,1995: 77). It is a paradigm shift that the contributors to this volume would welcome.

Unravelling the Semantics

Rather than attempting to pin down and distinguish between approaches to change in communities, some theorists have advocated use of the umbrella term "community work" (Wharf, 1979; Dominelli, 1989; and Reitsma-Street and Neysmith, 2000). In many ways this is a useful term and may indeed have been the term of choice for this book. However, because of the semantic confusion that would occur by using both community work and community social work, we have returned to Rothman's notion of community organization to describe locality development, social planning, social action, and social reform. We use "community social work" to describe practice that is family and community-centred, and we apply the term "community control" where communities have taken over responsibility for child welfare. When it is convenient to group these concepts together we use "community approaches."

As used here these community approaches are informed by analyses of class, race, and gender. They are political activities designed to assist second-class citizens, be they poor or members of an oppressed race or group, to become first-class citizens. Although Henderson uses the term "community development," his words capture our thinking: "Community development exists because it has a value based commitment to working with the excluded of society, those people who are too poor, too oppressed or too alienated to be confident about getting involved in community activities" (Henderson, 1997: 26).

The three approaches differ on the important dimension of control of practice. In community social work, control remains with the practitioner and the agency; in community organization, control is shared with residents and users of child welfare services; and community control refers to programs and practice that are the responsibility of the community. In addition the approaches build on one another. Thus, community organization practice contains the same attitude of respect for service users evident in community social work, and community control uses the strategies of community organization in a way that involves all members of the community in deciding how the developmental needs of children can best be met.

The activities of community approaches with specific reference to the welfare of children include working in communities to:

- locate programs in the community and tune these to meet its needs;

- develop community capacity to respond to situations of child neglect and abuse and on a more proactive basis to care for its children. Developing capacity includes establishing formal resources such as daycare, recreation, family places, and enhancing the ability of residents to assist each other;

- advocate for changes in the policies and programs of the state;

- gain control of resources and programs and provide these in a manner that involves citizens in the development and management of programs;

- address the issues of race, class, and gender;

- connect issues to those in other communities and to provincial and national social policies.

The responsibilities of community approaches can be assigned in different ways:

- as part of a generic workload of child welfare staff;

- as a full-time assignment for child welfare staff;

- as a full-time assignment for staff who work in a department or unit devoted to community organizing;

- as an integral part of the work of the agency. Such an approach is most likely to be found in community-controlled agencies.

What Do We Mean by Community?

One way of coming to grips with the elusive notion of community is to list the conditions that taken together identify a community:

- people have a sense of belonging;

- people have shared values and interests;

- some common goals can be identified;

- boundaries define the geographic location of the community;

- the people share common demographic characteristics such as race and class;

- the people have a sense of shared history.

But communities also differ markedly. One analytic framework distinguishes between neighbourhoods by assessing them according to three social dimensions:

- IDENTITY: How much do people feel they belong to a neighborhood and share a common destiny with others?

- INTERACTION: How often and with what number of neighbors do people interact on the average during the year?

- LINKAGES: What are the linkages to the larger community? Are there people who have memberships in outside groups or bring news about the larger community back into the neighborhood? (Warren, 1980: 69)

Using these dimensions Warren identified six types of neighbourhoods: integral, parochial, diffuse, stepping stone, transitory, and anomic. In an integral neighbourhood, individuals are in close contact with one another but also participate in activities outside the neighbourhood. Parochial neighbourhoods are distinctly different. They have a strong ethnic identity or homogenous character and are not interested in happenings in the outside world. Residents in diffuse neighbourhoods share many interests, but these commonalities do not lead to action. In stepping-stone neighbourhoods, people participate in activities but do so primarily because these are seen as ways of advancing careers. Transitory neighbourhoods are characterized by change, while anomic areas are essentially non-neighbourhoods with little social cohesion or interaction.

This framework identifies the strengths and limitations of neighbourhoods. Thus, stepping stone, transitory, and anomic areas lack internal cohesion and a sense of common purpose. Organizing these neighbourhoods to respond to child neglect and abuse will be much more difficult than in integral, parochial, and diffuse neighbourhoods. Yet, despite its potential usefulness to practitioners, the literature reveals few attempts to use this framework to identify the requirements needed for community work. One research project in Winnipeg (Fuchs, 1995) made conscious use of it; this project is noted below and in Chapter 4.

Before proceeding to a discussion of community approaches to child welfare, we briefly consider the significance of community in a world dominated by transnational corporations and an ethos of globalization. At a time when the attention of nations is focussed on international issues, does the local community matter? On the one hand, as noted throughout this book, neo-conservative governments view community as a convenience to offload the human service responsibilities of the state. For these governments global affairs are the priority, and offloading may well weaken community capacity. On the other hand, community may assume increased importance for citizens since it is a familiar, even comfortable, place that provides a sense of stability in a world that few ordinary citizens comprehend. "Shaped by such global and impersonal forces as the decomodification of labour, the community sector appears to provide an antidote to alienation, a structured space in which those excluded from the traditional work world can create meaning and a social identity" (White, 1994: 28). Seen from this perspective, globalization may promote the development of integral communities that can assume responsibility for child welfare, exert pressure on the state for required resources, and advocate for new approaches to practice.

Community Approaches and Child Welfare

Since child welfare agencies in Canada have made only sporadic attempts to use community approaches it comes as no surprise to learn that the literature is sparse. There is, however, an extensive literature on mutual aid and natural helping networks and on the contributions of family centres to child welfare. The following discussion outlines the literature on these two related matters and then turns to a review of the writings on community organizing in child welfare.

MUTUAL AID AND NATURAL HELPING NETWORKS
The literature on mutual aid and natural helping networks is voluminous and no attempt is made here to comment on the literature in the U.S. or other countries. Instead, we rely on two recent Canadian research projects that have direct reference to the welfare of children. The first concerns the work of Cameron, who with several colleagues developed parent mutual aid organizations in three Ontario Children's Aid Societies. The objective was to determine if creating social sup-

ports for parents would prevent out-of-home placements. The results of this project indicated that members of the mutual aid organizations "used care about one half to one third as frequently as the comparison sample" (Cameron, 1995: 70 to 71). Cameron's overall conclusion was that "the parent mutual aid organization intervention model may be able to respond in a substantial way to the problems of isolation and loneliness experienced by many families coming to child welfare agencies for help" (ibid.).

A second study conducted in Winnipeg in two inner-city neighbourhoods produced similar findings. This four-year project focussed on increasing the social supports for low-income families through both formal and informal means. The study concluded that "the risk for child maltreatment in a community can be reduced by social network intervention" (Fuchs, 1995: 121). The results of these two carefully designed projects parallel those achieved in numerous studies in other countries. (See, among others, Gottlieb, 1988; Whittaker and Garbarino, 1983; Garbarino, 1982). Speculation in this book as to why community organizing has remained on the periphery of practice in child welfare been matched by questions about the contribution of mutual aid not only in child welfare but in the human services in general. Many years ago one of the early advocates wrote that "mutual aid was an idea whose time had come" (Collins, 1981: viii). But in the intervening decades child welfare agencies have given only limited attention to mutual aid and natural helping networks, concentrating energies instead on more individual approaches, such as risk assessment.

COMMUNITY RESOURCE CENTERS, FAMILY RESOURCE PROGRAMS, AND NEIGHBOURHOOD HOUSES

A related stream of literature concerns the contributions of agencies that provide both user-friendly services and involve those receiving services in the development of programs and policies in the agency. Participation not only results in programs and policies tuned to the needs of those being served, but strengthens the confidence and self-image of these residents. These agencies are variously known as neighbourhood or settlement houses, family resource programs, and community resource centres—these titles are used interchangeably throughout the book. It may be argued that there are differences between these agencies. For example, throughout their history neighbourhood houses have emphasized the need for social reform while family resource programs tend to concentrate on providing services. But as the authors of a major study point out the "range of services offered by family resource programs varies depending on their stage of organizational development, their community context, their assessment of community needs and on available resources" (Kyle and Kellerman, 1998: 55). And differences also occur within neighbourhood houses, with some taking an active role in social reform while others have focussed on providing services.

While neighbourhood houses have existed for many years in some Canadian cities, the more recent interest in developing support programs for families has taken the form of family resource programs located in and administered by a variety of community agencies. The number of programs has grown to such an extent that a national association was formed to promote the work. The Canadian Association of Family Resource Programs is now engaged in a project that seeks to find the common ground between child welfare agencies and family support programs. The project is described in some detail in Chapter 6.

Some interesting insights have emerged from research on community resource centres. Reitsma-Street and Neysmith examined the work of three centres in the Better Beginnings Project established by the federal and the Ontario provincial governments. Started in 1991 this project aimed "to prevent future behavioural problems in at-risk children while promoting healthy development" (Reitsma-Smith and Neysmith, 2000: 43). Essentially, the projects used the approach of locality development to create programs needed in poor, urban neighbourhoods and in so doing to increase the capacity of residents to look after one another. Initially created with a five-year lifespan, the projects, eight in all, were given permanent but largely inadequate core funding when the initial time frame ended.

The majority of staff and those being served in the community resource centres were women and, not surprisingly, the researchers suggest that community work can be seen "as a type of caring labour that sustains the quality of people's lives in their daily, immediate world" (ibid., 146). The research identified four tasks in the community work performed in these centres: services, relationship-building, planning, and shadow activities. Services include the activities needed to meet daily needs such as playing with children, serving in the community kitchen, and organizing meetings and events. Relationship-building and planning are familiar tasks in community work, whereas shadow work refers to activities required to support more tangible tasks. "Participants spoke of grandmothers who babysat children so that they could come to meetings. Typical is the example where a child is only able to participate because another parent picks them up" (ibid, 150).

Long (1995: 64) from Save the Children, a voluntary organization that operates a number of family support centres in the U.K., typifies the philosophy of these agencies:

> Save the Children centres are not to be viewed within the crisis oriented mode of interventions which offer therapeutic help to families and children in need but are firmly based within the community development framework. They provide practical responses to locally defined need. The principles of open access, self referral and user participation are fundamental to this approach.

Because of these principles neighbourhood houses and family resource programs are viewed by the contributors to this book as being invaluable components in an overall network of services. Certainly our preference is for neighbourhood houses that assume responsibility for advocacy and social reform as well as the provision of services. Yet an irony of some moment is that in some provinces (for example, Ontario) neighbourhood houses have received financial support from governments dedicated to the reduction if not elimination of the welfare state. The appeal for neo-conservative governments is that neighbourhood houses with their extensive use of volunteers and commitment to people helping people are seen as a replacement for rather than as a support to other provincial and federal programs.

Community Organizing and Child Welfare

The Children's Aid Society of Toronto was the first child welfare agency in Canada to launch a community program, and the earliest articles to appear were written by staff members of this agency (Barr, 1971, 1979; Barr and McLaughlin, 1975). The agency placed child welfare workers in low-income neighbourhoods and workers divided their time between traditional child welfare responsibilities and community organizing. Initially they engaged in a locality development approach involving residents in determining the kind of resources and services they required and then participating in the management of these resources. But another and key contribution of these early workers is summed up by Barr (1979: 45):

> In essence the main innovation proposed in Regent Park was a new solution to old problems. Simply put it was the

residents would be involved not only defining but carrying out the changes required to solve their own problems. Seeing the client as a consumer of services with opinions as to how services might be more effectively delivered resulted in changing the definition of problems. For example family crises which had been looked upon as interpersonal communication problems by agency staff became viewed as short term economic crises which could be dealt with more effectively by providing material and financial services.

Involving those being served in defining and suggesting responses to their problems represented at that time—and still does today—a radical departure from traditional forms of practice. An innovation of this magnitude had the potential to alter the balance of power between professional social workers and their clients. After all, a large part of the professional body of knowledge and practice is concerned with forming expert diagnoses and treatment plans. The Regent Park and other initiatives seemed to many to surrender these professional tasks to those being served. Yet involvement does not necessarily mean surrender but rather partnership. As noted earlier, the delicate task of building effective partnerships that blend the respective knowledge and skills of both user and professional represents a challenge for social work that has not been resolved. And the absence of a resolution raises the question of whether social workers who are committed to a clinical approach that retains the responsibility for diagnosis and setting treatment plans must reject or at least not actively support community work approaches in child welfare.

The locality development approach has also characterized the community program in Winnipeg Family and Children's Services (Hudson, 1999; Chapter 4, this volume) and that of the Ministry of Social Services in B.C. (Swets, Rutman, and Wharf, 1995). While receiving positive reactions from many communities the latter initiative was cancelled abruptly and with no explanation after a scant two years. The community programs in Winnipeg and Toronto are still alive, but as Chapter 4 makes clear they represent only a minor part of their respective agencies.

While beginning with a locality development approach, community workers in the Toronto Children's Aid Society extended their activities to include social planning and social reform. Chapter 4 describes a number of activities undertaken by community workers in conjunction with residents and neighbourhood associations. These actions include preserving affordable housing, legalizing suites in houses, providing loans to low-income people to prevent eviction, establishing a comprehensive system of daycare, preparing briefs on social issues for the Board of Directors of the agency, and promoting community economic development.

A number of issues have been identified in the above discussion with reference to the viability of community organizing in child welfare. These include challenging the traditional one-to-one, office-based approach to practice and the professional expertise of social workers to diagnose and propose treatment plans. In addition, community organizing draws attention to the public issues of poverty and poor housing and is viewed by some as inappropriate meddling in political matters. The combination of these and other factors may account for the minor part community organization has played in the child welfare enterprise. These vexing issues are pursued in all of the following chapters.

Community Organization and Social Policy

As noted earlier, neo-conservative politicians are in the vanguard of championing a return to community care. In their vision communities are characterized by neighbours helping neighbours and by kindness and generosity towards all. In this view communities can manage quite well without the costly and initiative-sapping programs of the state. However, like families, communities can be a source of refuge and support, but they can also be places where intolerance and cruelty prevail. After all, if child neglect and abuse had not occurred in the past, it would not have been necessary for the state to establish legislation and child welfare agencies.

We are also aware that the condition of "acute localitis" can prevail in communities and particularly in parochial communities with only fragile ties to the rest of the country (Montgomery, 1979). Acute localitis refers to communities where leadership rests in the hands of a few individuals and where standards of behaviour differ substantially from those that have been established in the larger social system. Thus, while substantial arguments can be mounted to plead the case for community control of child welfare, such control must be placed within the overall context of provincial legislation, provincial standards, and provincial accrediting bodies.

An exception to this assertion relates to First Nation communities. In Chapter 5, the authors of case studies of Lalum'utul'Smun'eem and West Region argue that the exercise of provincial control over First Nation child welfare agencies thwarts their attempts to reverse the effects of colonialism and to build culturally appropriate programs. The argument is well taken, but in order to ensure that acute localitis does not occur some First Nation provincial and national organizations must take responsibility for developing appropriate standards and for the accreditation of First Nation programs.

The position of the contributors to this book is that communities cannot go it alone. Community control and capacity building must not provide policy-makers at federal and provincial levels with the opportunity to abdicate responsibility for human services. Some services, such as child welfare and outpatient health and mental health, can be provided best at the local level, but these will be most effective if they are nested within national/provincial programs for income security, unemployment insurance, low-cost housing, and medicare. Indeed, an as-yet unrealized social policy partnership could be developed between senior levels of government and communities. For example, the effects of national/provincial programs are most keenly felt at the community level: on the streets, in the schools, in recreation centres, and in the homes in local communities. Communities are in a unique position to comment on the adequacy and suitability of these programs. However, the most completely documented community research reports will be of little benefit to citizens if senior levels of government persist in their present pattern of ignoring social problems.

The Organization of the Book

With three exceptions the remaining chapters consist of case studies of community approaches in child welfare agencies and in the Black community in Nova Scotia. The exceptions are Chapters 2, 6, and 7. Chapter 2, "Getting to Now: Children in Distress in Canada's Past," is included in the collection for two reasons. First, it takes issue with the belief referred to above and still cherished by many individuals that communities of the past were always beneficent to children. Given the intent of the book to present a case for community approaches, a firm rejection of this romantic notion is required. Second, it argues that at a policy level "children need access to support that does not automatically designate any as inferior or abnormal," and this stance is consistent with and supports the philosophical position of community approaches.

Chapter 6 is devoted to "Searching for Common Ground" between family resource programs and child welfare agencies, while the final chapter summarizes the insights from the case studies and inquires whether community approaches can gain a more substantial presence in child welfare.

The case studies are presented in Chapters 3, 4, and 5. Chapter 3 outlines two examples of community social work approaches in the Ministry for Children and Families in B.C. Chapter 4 presents the community organization approaches of the Toronto Children's Aid Society and the Winnipeg Child and Family Services that developed comprehensive programs incorporating locality development, social planning, and social reform. Chapter 4 also includes the story of the attempts of the Association of Black Social Workers in Nova Scotia to develop culturally appropriate programs for Black children and families. Chapter 5 contains two case studies of First Nations agencies that have assumed responsibility for child welfare and have done so in a way that preserves cultural traditions and involves the entire community in caring for children and planning for the development of programs.

references

Absolon, K. and E. Herbert. 1997. "Community Action as a Practice of Freedom: A First Nations Perspective," in B. Wharf and M. Clague, eds., *Community Organizing: Canadian Experiences*. Toronto: Oxford University Press, 205-27.

Adams, P. and K. Krauth. 1995. "Working With Families and Communities: The Patch Approach," in P. Adams and K. Nelson, eds., *Reinventing Human Services, Community and Family Centered Practice*. New York: Aldine de Gruyter Inc., 87-08.

Alinsky, S. 1972. *Rules for Radicals*. New York: Vintage Books.

Barr, D. 1971. "Doing Prevention," *Ontario Association of Children's Aid Society Journal* (Feb.): 8-13.

———. 1979. "The Regent Park Community Service Unit: Partnership Can Work," in B. Wharf, ed., *Community Work in Canada*. Toronto: McClelland and Stewart, 27-50.

Barr, D. and A. McLaughlin. 1975. "A Community Worker Prevention Program," *Ontario Association of Children's Aid Society Journal* (April).

Batten, T.R. 1957. *Communities and Their Development*. London. Oxford University Press.

Burgess, J., R. Hern, and B. Wharf. 2000. "From Case and Client to Citizen: An Innovation in Child Welfare Practice," in M. Callahan and S. Hessle, eds., *Valuing the Field: Child Welfare in an International Context*. Aldershot, Hampshire: Ashgate Press, 99-116.

Callahan, M. 1997. "Feminist Community Organizing in Canada: Postcards from the Edge," in B. Wharf and M. Clague, eds., *Community Organizing: Canadian Experiences*. Toronto: Oxford University Press, 181-204.

Cameron, G. 1995. "The Nature and Effectiveness of Parent Mutual Aid Organizations in Child Welfare," in J. Hudson and B. Galaway, eds., *Child Welfare in Canada: Research and Policy Implications*. Toronto: Thompson Educational Publishing, 66-81.

Collins, F. 1981. "Preface," in C. Froland, D.L. Pancoast, N. Chapman, and P.J. Kimboko, eds., *Helping Networks and Human Services*. Beverley Hills. CA: Sage Publishing.

Dominelli, L. 1989. *Women and Community Action*. Birmingham: Venture Press.

Fuchs, D. 1995. "Preserving and Strengthening Families and Protecting Children: Social Network Intervention, a Balanced Approach to the Prevention of Child Maltreatment," in J. Hudson and B. Galaway, eds., *Child Welfare in Canada: Research and Policy Implications*. Toronto: Thompson Educational Publishing, 113-22.

Friere, P. 1985. *Pedagogy of the Oppressed*. New York: Continuum Publishing.

Garbarino, J. 1982. *Children and Families in the Social Environment*. New York. Aldine.

Gottlieb, B. 1983. *Social Support Strategies: Guidelines for Mental Health Strategies*. Beverley Hills, CA: Sage Publishing.

Gutierrez, G. 1983. *The Power of the Poor in History*. New York: Orbis Books.

Henderson, P. 1997. "Community Development and Children," in C. Caanan and C. Warren, eds., *Social Action with Children and Families, A Community Development Approach to Child and Family Welfare*. London: Routledge, 23-42.

Hudson, P. 1999. "Community Development and Child Protection: A Case for Integration," *Community Development Journal* 34, 4: 346-54.

Kyle, I., and M. Kellerman. 1998. *Case Studies of Canadian Family Resource Programs*. Ottawa: Canadian Association of Family Resource Programs.

Lee, B. 1999. "A Community Approach to Urban Child Welfare," in L. Dominelli, L., ed., *Community Approaches to Child Welfare*. Aldershot: Ashgate Press, 64-94.

Long, G. 1995. "Family Poverty and the Role of Family Support Work," in M. Hill, R.H. Kirk, and D. Part, eds., *Supporting Families*. Edinburgh: HMSO.

McKnight. J. 1995. *The Careless Society*. New York: Vintage Books.

Miller, S.M., M. Rein, and P. Levitt. 1990. "Community Action in the United States," *Community Development Journal* 25, 4: 356-68.

Montgomery, J. 1979. "The Populist Front in Rural Development: Or Shall We Eliminate the Bureaucrats and Get on with the Job?," *Public Administration Review* (Jan./Feb.): 58-65.

O'Brien, D. 1979. "Documentation of Social Need, A Critical Planning Activity: Variations on an Old Theme," in B. Wharf, ed., *Community Work in Canada*. Toronto: McClelland and Stewart, 225-41.

Perlman, R. and A. Gurin. 1972. *Community Organizing and Social Planning*. New York: John Wiley and Sons.

Reitsma-Street, M. and S. Neysmith. 2000. "Restructuring and Community Work: The Case of Community Resource Centres for Families in Poor Urban Neighbourhoods," in S. Neysmith, ed., *Restructuring Caring Labour*. Toronto: Oxford University Press, 142-63.

Ross, M. 1955. *Community Organization: Theory and Principles*. New York: Harper and Row.

Rothman, J. 1974. "Three Models of Community Organization Practice," in F. Cox, J. Tropman, J. Ehrlich, and J. Rothman, eds., *Strategies of Community Organization*. Itasca, IL: Peacock Press. 22-39.

Smale, G. 1995. "Integrating Community and Individual Practice: A New Paradigm for Practice," in P. Adams and K. Nelson, eds., *Reinventing Human Services, Community and Family Centered Practice*. New York: Aldine de Gruyter, 59-86.

Swets, R., D. Rutman, and B. Wharf. 1995. "The Community Development Initiative of the Ministry of Social Services." Victoria, B.C.: University of Victoria. School of Social Work, Child, Family and Community Research Program.

Warren, D. 1980. "Support Systems in Different Types of Neighbourhoods," in J. Garbarino, S. Stocking, and Associates, eds., *Protecting Children from Abuse and Neglect*. San Francisco: Jossey Bass.

Wharf, B. 1979. *Community Work in Canada*. Toronto: McClelland and Stewart.

——. 1993. *Rethinking Child Welfare in Canada*. Toronto: McClelland and Stewart.

Whittaker, J.K. and J. Garbarino. 1983. *Social Support Networks: Informal Helping in the Human Services*. New York: Aldine, 61-93.

2

Getting To Now:

Children In Distress In Canada's Past

VERONICA STRONG-BOAG

In order to understand the problems in child welfare that Canada confronts at the beginning of the twenty-first, it is helpful to remind ourselves of where we have been as a nation with regard to the care of children. This chapter sets out that longer perspective. It begins by pointing out that children in distress are nothing new. Some youngsters, especially those from less powerful groups, have always been in need of assistance beyond what their families can provide. The second section examines the changing views of children that have informed private philanthropy and public policy. Social workers, like Canadians in general, have been deeply influenced by shifting ideas about how much independence, protection, segregation, and responsibility girls and boys should have. The third section reviews the practices of early Canadian child-savers and suggests that control was as important as rescue. In a state that frequently valued waged over other kinds of labour and men over women, mother-led families were especially vulnerable. The final pages consider the benefits and the dangers of universal and targeted assistance. How, they ask, are children in need not to be further stigmatized? To better understand our history is to begin to answer that critical question.

A Problem with a Long History

Children in distress are not new. Nor are they, as today's reactionary commentators would have us believe, a particular product of contemporary forces, whether they be secularism, globalism, or feminism. Some families have always been unwilling or, which was far more often the case, unable to protect their offspring. Over time, death and disability, poverty and unemployment have injured many generations of children and in the process massively compromised the child-rearing capacities of their parents. Privilege and power of various kinds have sheltered some families and children. Women, the working class, those with disabilities, and non-dominant racial and ethnic groups in general, however, have regularly suffered great distress. Although a few communities, notably some First Nations, appear to be relatively child-friendly, historical evidence repeatedly shows us that always some youngsters have lived lives that were difficult, not to say impossible.

When biological families fail, extended kin or neighbours have sometimes been there to help, but it has been dangerously easy to romanticize those prospects in the past. There has never been a golden age of the family. While regularly subject in much of the world to patriarchal authority, families have nevertheless come in various shapes and sizes. They have had many different ties to communities and have offered a wide range of experiences to their members. Support for children, and adults for that matter, has always been likely to be highly contingent on good health, on physical proximity, on intimate relations, and on the relative social ranking of the children and their potential caregivers.

Canada has been no different. As the operation of the Poor Laws in early Nova Scotia and New Brunswick demonstrated, disease and premature death haunted much of Canadian history, compromising children's nurture in a host of ways. In the Maritime colonies, "the sick, the mentally ill, the mentally retarded, infants and children, tramps and vagrants," as well as the elderly, passed their days in almshouses or found themselves auctioned off to the lowest bidder who would house and feed them (Guest, 1980: 10). Upper Canada, later Ontario, rejected the Elizabethan Poor Law system in the expectation that frontier families and private charity could cope adequately with distress. This quickly proved no solution. Jails, asylums, and hospitals became the crowded refuges of the poor of all ages. Private charity and religious institutions provided equally cold comfort in colonial Quebec. Canada's long, harsh winters with their special threat to health, employment, and comfort in general made destitution and distress all the more difficult to survive in the New World (Fingard, 1974). Infant and child mortality was correspondingly high. With the union of the British North American colonies from 1867-73, the growth of industrialization and urbanization, the spread of European settlement into the West, and increasingly diverse patterns of immigration, older makeshift responses appeared even less adequate.

The Native nations that occupied northern North America have been diverse in their traditions and practices with regard to social hierarchy and gender as well as adult-child relations. Evidence of early child-rearing practices more gentle than those of Europeans is plentiful, as with the Montagnais-Naskapi in northern Labrador and the Plains Cree (Leacock, 1986; Van Kirk, 1980). Whether kindness determined the dominant experience of children is, however, yet unknown. Native legends, for example, sometimes suggest that children might not always have been equally or sensitively treated.[1] Whatever the state of pre-contact societies, the lives of Aboriginal youngsters, like those of adults generally, deteriorated with the arrival of Europeans. More and different diseases left unprecedented numbers of dead, orphaned, or injured. Resource depletion and loss brought more hunger and disability. Direct assaults on Aboriginal culture and traditions undermined long-standing obligations and exchanges. While their own nations were decreasingly able to nurture them, Native children had good reason to expect worse from settler society, which had little to offer the poor or the marginal of any race.

By the late nineteenth century children under age 15 made up some 40 per cent of a Canadian population that numbered about four million. All were vulnerable to disease and discipline in ways that are difficult to imagine at the start of the twenty-first century. Vulnerability was not shared equally. Then as now, gender, ethnicity, race, class, and ability determined children's options. While the precise number in distress is impossible to measure, surviving evidence suggests that many thousands of girls and boys experienced want and abuse on the road to adulthood. Their stories are only beginning to be told.

Changing Views of Children

The recurring historical documentation of young lives disfigured by poverty and disease, as well as by adult brutality and indifference, has encouraged some scholars to examine views of children even to the extent of asking whether past parents actually loved their offspring. While that question has been answered overwhelmingly in the affirmative (Cunningham, 1995), there is also substantial agreement that attitudes to children and childhood in the western world have changed markedly since the industrial revolution, in other words, over the last 250 years or so. Many factors were involved, notably the appearance of a more liberal Christianity, the growth in industrial and agricultural productivity, the rise of the middle class, the greater emancipation of women, and enlarged notions of citizenship. Patricia Rooke and Rudy Schnell (1983: 8) have usefully summed up the resulting ideal. Deeply rooted in bourgeois sensibilities, this "can be defined according to the four major criteria of 'dependence, protection, segregation, and delayed responsibilities.'" In other words, the ideal children of the modern age were expected to count on adults to meet their basic needs; their bodies and minds were to be defended, especially from older predators; they should be assisted and treated separately from grown-ups; and they should not have to work, particularly outside the home, until maturity.

The shift in prevailing sentiment from an emphasis on children as immature adults to a special category of human beings with considerable potential for good and to whom the community had special obligations was gradual and piecemeal. Liberal assumptions about the nature of children and childhood always confronted older views that emphasized "the Adam in man" or "spare the rod and spoil the child." From the beginning and into the twenty-first century harsher views have applied also far more to the offspring of socially dominant groups than others. Nevertheless, new ideas about children pervade modern sensibilities and represent one of the most consequential developments in world history. As enshrined today in the United Nations Declaration on the Rights of the Child (1989), the singling out of the young for special attention has become one of the critical benchmarks of civilized society.

Increasingly influenced by humanized visions of Jesus and the Virgin Mary, Canada's nineteenth- and early twentieth-century Protestant and Catholic pulpits provided influential platforms for new ideas. Sunday schools and religious children's and youth groups regularly brought the children's gospel into homes everywhere. Protestant support for temperance societies, like the Woman's Christian Temperance Union, spread the same message throughout the Dominion (Cook, 1995). Much of the thrust of the "social gospel" (a term that encompasses early twentieth-century Christian churches' efforts to tackle the social problems of the times) was inspired directly by the determination to bring children's lives more in tune with humane ideals (Allen, 1971).

Middle-class women, many themselves evangelical Christians, were leaders in demanding a better deal for children. In the course of constructing their own claims to emancipation from patriarchal authority, reform-minded women readily emphasized their role as mothers. Their sex was, many feminists argued and many more agreed, innately equipped to nourish youngsters to their full potential. Campaigns for equality in custody and divorce, in education and employment, not to mention

for suffrage and full citizenship generally, were readily justified by reference to the better fulfillment of maternal duties in the private home
and in the world at large. Once liberated from the handicaps of male
authority and prejudice, female activists looked forward to an important role in overseeing and guaranteeing the more humane treatment
of youngsters (Prentice et al., 1988).

Changing ideas about women, the social purpose of religion, and
the nature of children powerfully influenced the so-called "helping
professions" of nursing/medicine, teaching, and social work. All played
a significant role in the development of welfare services. Social workers, the majority of whom have always been female, staffed a growing
variety of private and public services beginning in the nineteenth century. Pioneer professionals, like Canadians generally, shifted uneasily
between ideas that stressed individual responsibility and those that
emphasized the structural problems of unemployment and poverty. On
the front line of community response to children in distress, social
workers struggled from the beginning to construct strategies that would
accommodate Canadians' growing idealism about children with the
reality of inadequate funds. Case work, like the battery of personality
and mental tests in use, became increasingly part of the social work
arsenal in the twentieth century. In the course of individualizing the
problem child, such methods appeared to make social work both scientific and practical. Whatever assistance such approaches promised,
they also directed attention away from questions of systemic inequal-
ity. Although Canadian social workers have always been among the
foremost champions of a fair deal for children, they have also been
employed to supervise programs that did little to bridge the gap between
an ideal environment and the harsh reality of youngsters' existence.

Reconsideration of children's nature and treatment benefitted significantly from the emergence of the mass circulation press in the
Victorian Age. The explosion of child-awareness in popular literature
of every sort offered unprecedented opportunities to mobilize public
opinion. Best-selling novelists like Charles Dickens and Lucy Maud
Montgomery helped readers around the world develop greater sym-
pathy and closer identification with the children in their midst. Canada's
best-known literary juvenile is undoubtedly the orphan Anne of Green
Gables. The book of the same name, first published in 1908 and repub-
lished many times, dramatically conveys the hope of the new vision.
Here was a spirited young girl, much like Pearlie Watson in Nellie
McClung's *Saving Seeds for Danny*, another popular volume of the same
year, or the Native, mixed-race, and British boys championed by E.

Pauline Johnson in her short stories collected in *The Shagganappi* (1913). Such fictional youngsters embodied a better world in which poverty and disadvantage could be overcome. They suggested that the Dominion need not repeat the errors of the past. It could start fresh leaving behind history's tragic waifs and orphans. The popularity of Anne and her fictional contemporaries stemmed in large part from their happy prospects and those they implicitly promised for the young folk of the new land.

In fact, the experience of Montgomery's creation as an exploited little maid-of-all-work before she met Marilla and Matthew Cuthbert was far more commonplace. The healthy, attractive, and articulate child of respectable white parents, Anne, like Pearlie, was unusually fortunate. While Johnson's lads often have to battle racism, they, too, were an enormously talented lot, largely supported by understanding parents and enlightened Anglo-Celtic patriarchs. They had merely to be given a hearing to discover effective champions for their innate virtues. The solutions to predicaments threatening at the onset of the stories are ultimately overwhelmingly individual. Except for occasional brief interludes, as when Anne is in an orphanage, such children largely escaped notice from the private and public welfare authorities. Indeed, there was little sign of formal child-savers at work, whether in juvenile reformatories or children's aid societies. Working out their fate in highly personal ways, the sentimental heroines and heroes beloved by readers moved readily into adulthood without requiring their society to consider or address the condition of underprivileged youngsters in general. In this dimension they also reinforced dogmas of *laissez-faire* liberalism and social Darwinism that insisted on personal responsibility and left little room for collective solutions to social problems.

Real children had good reason to envy their fictional counterparts. Many Canadian children fared far worse. The heart-wrenching stories of pauper immigrants and Native abductions described by Joy Parr in *Labouring Children* (1994) and Suzanne Fournier and Ernie Crey, Jr., in *Stolen from Our Embrace* (1997) document the more common reality. Recurring patterns of neglect and psychological, physical, and sexual abuse, echoed further in a host of royal commissions and public and private investigations, such as the 1889 *Report* of the Royal Commission on the Relations of Capital and Labour and the 2000 *Report, Protecting Our Students. A Review to Identify and Prevent Sexual Misconduct in Ontario Schools*, demonstrate that real life has rarely been as rosy as popular fiction would tempt us to believe. A mass of historical evidence, while of little surprise to those who actually work in the field of child welfare, has been regularly ignored by Canadian scholars (Strong-Boag,

1994). Even poverty, the bane of many lives, which Canadian legisla-
tors promised in 1991 to eliminate among young citizens, has been of
only episodic interest (Strong-Boag, 2000).

Yet if sentimental stories have misled readers, they also offered "scope
for the imagination" as Anne herself might say; in their pages, another
future might be glimpsed. Their role in helping to create a constituency
of support for more humane attitudes and even practices is ultimately
incalculable. In the nineteenth century religious leaders, activist women,
and amateur and professional social workers set out upon their child-
saving crusades amid a citizenry that was prepared, as never before, to
consider changing their ideas and practices regarding the care of children. The result was the creation of new private and public groups,
institutions, and tactics mobilized both formally and informally to transform the lives of children in distress.

While honoured too often more in theory than in practice, child-
savers' beliefs in dependence, protection, segregation, and delayed
responsibilities have been themselves far from unproblematic. The ideology they embody, rooted as it is in the Enlightenment and the evangelical history of the West, carries with it, unwittingly or not, corrosive
assumptions of superiority—of men over women, of the middle over
other classes, of European over other races, not to mention of age over
youth and of supposed ability over disability. As John Willinsky has
aptly demonstrated of education in his *Learning to Divide the World*
(1998), imbedded prejudices deeply compromise the inheritance of the
imperial West. In particular, the prejudices of the dominant belief system
have regularly encouraged many Canadian child-savers, whether private philanthropists, professional social workers, or reform-minded citizens in general, to be blind, both to collective injuries, whether they
be of gender, race, or class, and to the merits of other communities.
Not surprisingly, such myopia favours techniques, such as case work,
but also psychologizing of all sorts, that pathologize the individual. In
contrast, community development approaches that require a panoramic
perspective on children in distress struggle to combat a normative vision
of the world that resists institutional change as a matter of course since
it largely takes for granted the inferiority of others.

Since the nineteenth century Canadian children have lived increasingly with a legacy that emphasizes and celebrates their difference from
adults. The same inheritance that offers hope also makes critical distinctions among the young themselves. Some, those closest in character and potential to society's powerful élites, regularly receive the fullest
benefits of shifting sensibilities. White, able-bodied, attractive young-

sters have been permitted the longest and the greatest degree of dependence, protection, segregation, and delayed responsibilities. Less privileged youngsters would have to compare their very different experiences with what they read about Anne of Green Gables or saw of her equally atypical successors, increasingly mass-marketed in magazines, books, music, and on TV and movie screens. Native and disabled youngsters are representative of the large numbers who have frequently found it hard and unwise to depend on adults. As the revelations from Native residential schools and institutions for the deaf and the blind document in detail, children segregated in instruction and accommodation frequently have been abused. Responsibility for making their way in the world largely unaided by adults was likely to come especially early for offspring of the less powerful. Such unfortunates have in large part yet to inherit the beneficial legacy of the new ideas about childhood that emerged to mobilize Canadians in the nineteenth century.

Nineteenth-Century Child-Saving

In the second half of the nineteenth century child-saving assumed unprecedented dimensions. The young Dominion joined much of the western world in a wide-ranging series of private and public initiatives, from Protestant orphanages and Indian Residential Schools to Children's Aid Societies and legislation regarding child labour and compulsory schooling. New practices and policies designed for what were feared to be growing numbers of dependent, delinquent, and neglected youngsters emerged in the context of substantial shifts in gender relations, inter-class conflict, ethnic tensions, and Aboriginal resistance (Conrad, Finkel, and Strong-Boag, 1993). Led by middle-class women, ambitious churchmen, and socially-conscious professionals in law, education, medicine, and social work, more and more Canadians accepted special provisions for children as the key to the creation of a modern nation. At their best, innovations were intended to produce the "land of the fair deal" envisioned by feminists such as Nellie McClung (McClung, 1972). Like so many Pied Pipers, high-minded reformers in every province and territory set out to transport youngsters into a better world set safely apart from greedy, brutal, and ignorant adults. By 1921, in their determination to improve public health (e.g., through vaccinations and prenatal care), to identify and protect juvenile offenders (e.g., the Juvenile Delinquents Act 1908), to curb child labour (e.g., Factories, Shops, and Mines Acts of 1884, 1888, and 1890), and to humanize schooling (e.g., the New Education movement), Canada's child-centred champions had created "the chance of a fuller, richer life" for many young Canadian youngsters (Sutherland, 1976: 239).

Early efforts are, however, much more complicated in their motivation than any simple enumeration of vaccinated arms or rising literacy or falling infant mortality rates would have us believe. Child-saving lay at the heart of efforts to direct and discipline a multi-class and multi-ethnic state in which subordinated groups were demanding a voice. The years from Confederation to World War I constituted a tumultuous period of competing claims. The crises wrought by urbanization, immigration, and industrialization mobilized thousands in petitions, associations, strikes, and, occasionally, in pitched battles. Women denounced governments and laws that ignored their interests. Aboriginal peoples protested the denial of their rights in European Canada's rush for western and northern resources. Workers insisted that businessmen reaped unfair advantage from technological change and an immigration-fuelled labour market. National and local élites were on the firing line, forced to defend or to improve the status quo.

Children's rights, in effect the rights of different groups of children, were central to many conflicts. Native parents objected to residential schools; feminists targeted the abuse of girls; workers demanded better education for their children. Yet, for all the fundamental questions all asked about justice and fairness, such critics were rarely allies of one another. Whether Natives, feminists, or workers, they often pursued their particular battles, ignoring the misfortunes of others and unable or unwilling to look beyond their own ranks. The offspring of the most marginalized citizens continued to suffer as the élite of a post-settler society readily channelled genuine humanitarian impulses into programs that ultimately did little to threaten existing social relations.

Instead, explanations and solutions for poverty, disease, and mistreatment criticized as a matter of course the parenting qualifications of single mothers, of the First Nations, of non-Anglo-Celtic communities, and of the working class in general. Failure to measure up to normative standards that were overwhelming European, middle-class, and able-bodied, not to mention male, was ascribed to individual and community shortcomings rather than to the logic of the economic and social systems. Since the discipline of the marketplace was largely assumed to offer the best incentive to self-improvement, assistance rarely threatened to compromise fundamentally its imperatives. While girls and boys might be admitted to be the unfortunate casualties of parental incompetence and misfortune, the vast majority of help was intended to succour the needy at a level below that secured by the lowest-waged adult male worker. The iron rule of "lesser eligibility" ensured that children, no more than adults, were unable to escape the stern "law" of the survival of the fittest.

To be sure, children and their mothers presented a special dilemma. First of all, they made up the majority of those in distress in the nineteenth century and later on as well. As Bettina Bradbury has so well demonstrated in her study of nineteenth-century Montreal, mother-led families were only too likely to find themselves in desperate straits. The same story was repeated in every jurisdiction. Traditions of property-holding, domestic violence, and legal inferiority handicapped women and their heirs (Backhouse, 1991). Even when it was available, waged employment consistently favoured adult males, and businesses, unions, and governments ensured that this remained for the most part unchanged for much of Canada's history.

Feminist middle-class activists and their clerical and other allies responded to the tragedies around them by demanding social and legal recognition of women's primary role as parents and men's responsibilities as breadwinners. Working-class clients of initiatives such as Mothers' Pensions, beginning during World War I, were similarly insistent on winning acknowledgement of their claims to state support for parental duties (Christie, 2000: 9). This maternalist interpretation of citizenship, with its demand for official recognition for mothers' work in the creation of moral and responsible adults, floundered, however, during the 1930s. That particularly harsh decade saw mothers' rights largely superseded by "a set of entitlements founded on the workplace rights of men" (ibid.: 12). By World War II "motherhood no longer constituted an independent claim on the State," while "waged labour" won the battle to become the "fundamental criterion for welfare entitlements" (ibid: 253). That defeat was critical to the modern system of child welfare, which proceeded to evolve from familial to state patriarchy (Ursel, 1992), and in the process decisively to gender "definitions of citizenship rights and welfare entitlements" (Christie, 2000: 16).

Today's mothers and children continue to receive state benefits in very large part because individual men are viewed as failing in their fundamental role as breadwinners. Women's rights as social citizens are effectively mediated through their relationship to males, whose meaningful citizenship is in turn tied to their success in the economic market. The social entitlement of women and their offspring is compromised when they fail to maintain adult male support. Given the emphasis on individual responsibility, it comes as no surprise that female social welfare recipients have been commonly expected to demonstrate that the moral failure that caused them to seek aid was not theirs but rather that of a delinquent (whether by accident or design) male breadwinner. In order to receive secure benefits Canadian women historically have had to demonstrate moral fitness (Little, 1998). This has required their submission to externally imposed standards of conduct, with regard to everything from housekeeping to sexuality. Ultimately, only acquiescence confirmed their right to claims against the state. Just as men who rejected the constraints of the paid workplace could lose their jobs, recalcitrant women could lose benefits and, potentially, children. In other words, as Nancy Christie has recently demonstrated, women's claims to social rights and citizenship have been negotiated through their performance as wives and mothers. The Canadian child welfare system, with its recurring preference for the investigation of morality over practical support, is one continuing proof of women's general subordination as citizens.

The labour market's active discrimination in favour of the culturally dominant and against those marginalized by class, race/ethnicity, and disability has similarly direct consequences for children. Vulnerable families have been hard put to gain economic security. Parenting has been made immeasurably more difficult by inadequate wages, unsafe working conditions, and lack of economic opportunity generally. Taken-for-granted discrimination in the marketplace has helped ensure the need for child welfare. The move to universal public education, for all its promise, has not always improved matters. So-called scientific measurement, as with IQ testing, academic streaming (Gleason, 1999), and the meanest kind of vocational training (Miller, 1996), has consigned Native and other marginalized children to second-class citizenship in waged and unwaged workplaces. When contributions to the paid labour market became the central basis for claims of full citizenship, as manifested in eligibility for social security ranging from old age pensions to maternity benefits, a wide range of families and their offspring became casualties. Social assistance, both private and public, has been left to address their devastation.

The inability of many birth families to measure up on their own has produced two major responses to succouring children in distress. On the one hand, parents—most commonly mothers—and children have been monitored and supported at home, whether through private charity or public allowances. Continuation of "outdoor relief," whether it be pensions or vouchers, has depended on satisfactory behaviour. It has very rarely permitted any degree of comfort or promoted self-respect. The alternative has been the removal of the child or children, whether at the request of families themselves or mandated by external authority.

Impoverished parents or those unable to control their offspring have sometimes employed emigration societies, orphanages, and reformatories to help manage. For the most part, they have had hopes for restoring kin ties when matters improve (Bradbury, 1993; Parr, 1994). Some such strategies worked, as with Montreal widows retrieving children from St. Alexis Orphanage when better times returned; others like the desperate mothers who handed children over to the Barnardo organization more often failed. Early recognition of the problems associated with institutional life, especially for non-Native, non-delinquent, and disabled children, as well as its expense, provoked continuing interest in other alternatives. The Children's Aid Societies set up first in 1893 in Ontario and their subsequent imitators all across the country reflected the growing interest in fostering and adoption. But these too revealed their own problems. Good homes were always fewer than needed. Some children shifted from one site of mistreatment to another, often without hope of redress. The now infamous "scoop" of Native children from impoverished homes in the 1960s illustrated only too well how policies meant to sidestep institutions could be every bit as arbitrary and damaging as residential schools or Poor Law refuges. A variety of intermediary solutions—group homes are one example—have also been tried. At the beginning of the twenty-first century, child welfare experts acknowledge the benefits of keeping families together. However, as many of the following chapters argue, the laudable objective of protecting children and supporting families has yet to be realized.

Universal and Targeted Assistance

Right from the beginning Canadian experiments in child welfare can be broadly divided into two types: the universal and the particular. On the one hand, the post-Confederation years inaugurated major programs in public education and health that addressed the lot of all children. A massive expansion, first of primary and then of secondary schools, which became increasingly both free and compulsory through to the teenage years, brought unprecedented opportunities. This was far from unwelcome. Working-class, immigrant, and Native children and parents have a long history of using public education to advance personal and collective interests. Poor clients regularly used mothers' pensions and allowances after World War I and family allowances after World War II to prolong periods of schooling (Christie, 2000; Marshall, 1998). Tribal leaders like the Ojibway Shingwauk repeatedly demanded access to the best that education had to offer (Miller, 1996). By the end of the nineteenth century new options had helped produce a generation of Native, working-class, and feminist leaders who were better educated than ever before.

After Confederation advances in bacteriology and public health also rescued countless children and their parents from early death and disability. Communicable diseases, especially smallpox, diphtheria, tuberculosis, and typhoid, ceased to be inevitable hazards. With the beginning of the twentieth century most Canadian cities and increasing numbers of rural areas benefitted from visiting and public health nurses, including the Victorian Order of Nurses. They joined school nurses and public health inspectors to nurture juvenile minds and bodies. For the first time in human history large numbers of the disadvantaged began to learn what it meant to anticipate relatively good health and old age (Sutherland, 1976).

Yet, for all the undeniable progress, supposedly universal entitlement to schooling and fundamental medical care has been regularly compromised. Special treatment, regulated access, and individual prejudice have been constant. Working-class and Native girls have routinely been directed to training, whether in commercial or domestic subjects, that limited their options as adults (Gaskell, 1982; Miller, 1996). Poor children who came hungry or poorly clothed to classes frequently found little to keep them in attendance. The worst-off students have been unlikely to stay long enough or do well enough to make a critical difference to their futures. After the first great advances in public health and the inauguration of hospital and health insurance after World War II, disparity between the haves and have-nots has grown. Native and working-class youngsters, for example, are typically much more likely to go without a range of therapies, from psychiatry to ophthalmology, which promise help. Nor is that all. Right from the beginning, more powerful Canadians have routinely and for the great part unquestioningly supplemented universal entitlements with everything from private lessons to vitamins and summer camps. Theirs is a topped-up universality.

Much of the appeal of universal programs lay in their presumption of equality of opportunity. In fact poverty and its prejudices ensure no such outcome. The failure of most early and late campaigners in education and health to target impoverishment generally has undercut even the most well-intentioned of initiatives (Comacchio, 1993). The ground on which Canadians stood to receive entitlements, from free schooling to free vaccinations, remained pitted and uneven. At all times, many have lacked the safety net of family income and status that give second chances and enriched access to the more favoured of their peers.

The principle of universality, of a standard supposedly offered to all citizens has, however, been extraordinarily powerful. Native and immigrant parents, the mothers and fathers of special-needs children, the parents of girls, all groups variously subject to marginalization of one form or another, have at various times insisted on accountability from education and health-care systems. While their visions of an inclusive citizenship firmly grounded in equal access have often been betrayed, public schooling and health programs, from their inauguration in the nineteenth century, have offered underprivileged children their closest experience of equality with their age-mates. Current threats to universality from charter schools and fee-for-service medical services, on the other hand, compromise historic commitments to meeting the needs of all children as well as Canadians of all ages. In effect, they affirm and reify different categories of social citizenship.

The history of particular, segregated, or targeted programs—those, in other words, intended for other people's children—reveals the danger of recent assaults on the fundamental principle of universality. Children and their parents who have been variously designated as "other," as deviating in one or more crucial ways from the ideal, have been readily stigmatized and devalued. Whatever their good intentions, Canada's specialized child welfare initiatives, such as orphanages, residential schools for First Nation children, reformatories for those designated delinquent, day nurseries for the poor, shelters for unwed mothers, and group homes for troubled adolescents, have too often contributed to further victimization.

The historic problems created by segregated populations of children have been summed up in the Law Commission of Canada in *Restoring Dignity: Responding to Child Abuse in Canadian Institutions* (2000). This report describes how authorities ranging from parents and legal guardians to courts and child welfare agencies have consigned children to a wide variety of residential programs. Housed in total institutions by those "that seek to re-socialise people by instilling them with new roles, skills or values ... [in which] every aspect of his or her life is determined and controlled," such children have been consistently mistreated (ibid.: 22). The four categories of institutions singled out by the Commission— "special needs schools; child welfare facilities; youth detention facilities; and residential schools for Aboriginal children" (ibid.: 27)—have histories dating from the late nineteenth century.

While youngsters with special or developmental needs, those whose parents are unable or unwilling to offer a suitable level of care, those charged with offences, ranging from truancy to serious crime, and Aboriginal children in general have occasionally met sympathetic and helpful adults, all too often they have encountered abuse. Inmates of St. John's Mount Cashel orphanage, New Westminster's Woodlands Institution for the Mentally Handicapped, the Mimico Training School for Girls, the Prince Albert Indian Residential School, and the Quebec institutions that housed the Duplessis orphans regularly experienced physical and psychological isolation, degradation, including physical and sexual abuse, and their own powerlessness in face of arbitrary authority. Such casualties of the child welfare system are not anybody's children. Almost without exception, they are drawn historically from very disadvantaged populations.

Abusers have been quick to take advantage of children's lack of power. One example from Newfoundland's Mount Cashel (ibid.: 32) is typical:

> J.L. testified that some weeks before the first incident of sexual abuse by Kenny, the latter read the boy's family file to him. It referred to how the boy had been put in the orphanage because none of his relatives wanted him.
>
> J.L. stated that at one point in time Kenny told him he was a piece of garbage and that nobody wanted him. The boy said at that point he felt exactly like a piece of garbage. The incidents started not long after that.

Canada's institutionalized children have a history of resistance to such abuse. Long before the report of the Law Commission, orphanages, residential schools, and other institutions produced runaways, sabotage, active and passive disobedience, formal protests, fighting back, and suicides. While especially dramatic cases occasionally drew public attention and some children found adult champions, general recognition of the too-often tragic state of children in care waited until the late twentieth century. Only then, as the various recommendations of *Restoring Dignity* indicate, did Canadians begin to face up to the need for redress and criminal prosecution.

Yet, as the Law Commission recognizes, the necessity for institutions for children is never likely to disappear entirely. Some Canadian youngsters will always require assistance from beyond their family of origin. Children cannot always safely live with their own families or sometimes in families of any sort. In some cases appropriate foster parents are not available. Alternatives, however, are often far from obvious or likely to be quick in coming. They require an unprecedented willingness on the part of the larger community to accept youngsters in distress as collectively theirs, full citizens with equal rights.

At a minimum, this change in perception requires two shifts in attitude and practice. First, children need access to support that does not automatically designate any as inferior or abnormal. Guaranteed annual income, publicly funded daycare, and inclusive schooling would provide a good start. Second, children who, despite the adoption of genuinely family-friendly state policies, are nonetheless in distress should not be once again stigmatized by being further singled out. They need to find relief in a system that acknowledges universal risk and accepts that equal citizenship may require very different treatment. That response, with the additional resources it may very well necessitate, should not itself further confirm inferiority. In other words, children at risk, the vast majority of whom come from long-disadvantaged populations, need to be dealt with as if they were the offspring of policy-makers and service-providers. To make this change, Canadians and would-be child-savers will have to reconsider a long history in which gender, race/ethnicity, class, and ability have almost automatically consigned some of our young to conditions that are only too likely to produce tragedy. The time is overdue for all of Canada's children to benefit from that singular shift in thinking about children that occurred many decades ago. Until then our present as well as our past will provide ample evidence of children in distress.

note ———————————————————————————

1. See, for example, the treatment of a nephew in "The Gifts of the Little People," Burgeron (1985).

references ———————————————————————————

Allen, R. 1971. *The Social Passion: Religion and Social Reform in Canada, 1914-28.* Toronto: University of Toronto Press.

Backhouse, C. *Petticoats and Prejudice: Women and the Law in Nineteenth-Century Canada*. Toronto: Women's Press for the Osgoode Society.

Bradbury, B. 1993. *Working Families: Age, Gender, and Daily Survival in Industrializing Montreal*. Toronto: McClelland and Stewart.

Burgeron, J. 1985. *The Iroquois Stories*. Freedom, CA: The Crossing Press.

Canada, Law Commission. 2000. *Restoring Dignity: Responding to Child Abuse in Canadian Institutions*. Ottawa: Queen's Printer.

Christie, N. 2000. *Engendering the State: Family, Work, and Welfare in Canada*. Toronto: University of Toronto Press.

Comacchio, C.R. 1993. *"Nations are Built of Babies": Saving Ontario's Mothers and Children*. Montreal and Kingston: McGill-Queen's University Press.

Conrad, M., and A. Finkel, with V. Strong-Boag. 1993. *A History of the Canadian Peoples*, vol. 1. Toronto: Copp Clark Pitman.

Cook, S.A. 1995. *"Through Sunshine and Shadow": The Woman's Christian Temperance Union, Evangelicalism, and Reform in Ontario, 1874-1930*. Montreal and Kingston: McGill-Queen's University Press.

Cunningham, H. 1995. *Children and Childhood in Western Society since 1500*. London and New York: Longman.

Fingard, J. 1974. "'The Winter's Tale': The Seasonal Contours of Pre-Industrial Poverty in British North America, 1815-1860," Canadian Historical Association, *Historical Papers*, 65-94.

Fournier, S. and E. Crey, Jr. 1997. *Stolen from our Embrace: The Abduction of First Nations Children and the Restoration of Aboriginal Communities*. Vancouver: Douglas and McIntyre.

Gaskell, J. 1982. *Gender Matters from School to Work*. Philadelphia: Open University Press.

Gleason, M. 1999. *Normalizing the Ideal: Psychology, Schooling, and the Family in Postwar Canada*. Toronto: University of Toronto Press.

Guest, D. 1980. *The Emergence of Social Security in Canada*. Vancouver: University of British Columbia Press.

Leacock, E. 1986. "Montagnais Women and the Jesuit Program for Colonization," in A.C. Fellman and V. Strong-Boag, *Rethinking Canada: The Promise of Women's History*. Toronto: Copp Clark Pitman.

Little, M.J.H. 1998. *"No car, no radio, no liquor permit": The Moral Regulation of Single Mothers in Ontario, 1920-1997*. Toronto: Oxford University Press.

McClung, N.L 1972. *In Times Like These*. Toronto: University of Toronto Press.

Marshall, D. 1998. *Aux origines sociales de l'état-providence*. Montreal: Les presses de l'université de Montréal.

Miller, J.R. 1996. *Shingwauk's Vision: A History of Native Residential Schools.* Toronto: University of Toronto Press.

Parr, J. 1994. *Labouring Children: British Immigrant Apprentices to Canada, 1869-1924.* Toronto: University of Toronto Press.

Prentice, A., et al. 1988. *Canadian Women: A History.* Toronto: Harcourt Brace Jovanovich.

Rooke, P.T. and R.L. Schnell. 1983. *Discarding the Asylum: From Child Rescue to the Welfare State in English-Canada, 1800-1950.* Lanham, MD: University Press of America.

Strong-Boag, V. 1994. "Contested Space: The Politics of Canadian Memory," *Journal of the Canadian Historical Association* 5: 3-17.

——. 2000. "Long Time Coming: The Century of the Canadian Child?" *Journal of Canadian Studies* 35,1:124-37.

Sutherland, N. 1976. *Children in English-Canadian Society: Framing the Twentieth-Century Consensus.* Toronto: University of Toronto Press.

Ursel, J. 1992. *Private Lives, Public Policy: 100 Years of State Intervention in the Family.* Toronto: Women's Press.

Van Kirk, S. 1980. *Many Tender Ties: Women in Fur Trade Society in Western Canada, 1670-1830.* Winnipeg: Watson and Dwyer.

Willinsky, J. 1998. *Learning to Divide the World: Education at Empire's End.* Minneapolis: University of Minnesota Press.

3
Community Social Work in Two Provinces

Chapter 3 contains case studies of community social work approaches in B.C., and Quebec. All of the case studies are initiatives that capture the essence of community social work. They are family-centred and community-based and responsive, but do not as a continuing and priority activity include locality development, social planning, social action, or social reform.

part one

THE NEIGHBOURHOOD HOUSE PROJECT IN VICTORIA AND THE HAZELTON OFFICE OF THE MINISTRY FOR CHILDREN AND FAMILIES

BRIAN WHARF

The first part of the chapter tells the story of two approaches implemented by child welfare workers of the Ministry for Children and Families in B.C. One takes the form of a project where family-protection workers from a downtown office in Victoria have been placed in neighbourhood houses throughout the city. The second represents the ongoing work of a small office in the rural community of Hazelton.

In B.C. as in many other provinces, the statutory responsibilities for child welfare have been assigned to provincial ministries or departments. The only exception to this traditional and dominant pattern is that statutory responsibilities have been awarded to a few First Nation band and tribal councils. While there may well be other offices of the B.C. ministry that have adopted a community-based approach to practice, the two covered here were selected because of the author's relationships with key staff members. Riley Hern, the team leader of the

Victoria project, and I have worked together in a number of ways, including teaching a class on child welfare policy in the School of Social Work at the University of Victoria. I had visited the Hazelton office in connection with another research study and had established a good relationship with staff in this office (Callahan et al., 1998).

It is important to note at the outset that there is a significant difference between the roles assigned to staff in the two offices. As in other rural offices, staff in Hazelton are responsible for the full range of child welfare services, including investigating complaints of neglect and abuse, providing support to families, recruiting foster homes, and supervising the children in the care of these homes. By contrast, in urban offices like Victoria these responsibilities are divided among a number of specialized units: adoption and guardianship, foster home recruitment, investigation of complaints of neglect and abuse, and protection/family support. While formal complaints of child abuse and neglect are dealt with by investigation teams, the ongoing responsibility of monitoring the care of children is vested in the protective family support worker. The consequences of this division of responsibility are explored in a later section of the chapter.

The information for this chapter was obtained by visits to both offices. The interviews were taped and a draft of the account was sent to the offices to verify accuracy and comprehensiveness. The drafts were then combined and sent to the offices for comment and approval.

Neighbourhood Houses and Child Welfare

The project in Victoria had a long gestation period. In 1995, at a conference convened to discuss the implementation of new legislation, the supervisor of the project, the director of a neighbourhood house, and I identified the advantages to be gained by placing child welfare staff in neighbourhood houses throughout the city (Burgess, Hern, and Wharf, 2000).We thought that these locations would enable staff to become acquainted with families and their circumstances in a way that is virtually prohibited by office-bound practice. While both senior ministry staff and neighbourhood house directors gave early approval to the idea, implementation was delayed for nearly three years. During this time the ministry was preoccupied with a host of far-reaching changes brought about by the decision of the provincial government to approve many of the recommendations of a judicial inquiry into the death of a child.

The project located five protective family support workers in neighbourhood houses. The initial intent was that connections with their ministry office and record-keeping responsibilities would be maintained through laptop computers and cell phones. However, this intent has never been fully realized, in part because of the difficulty of securing this equipment on the somewhat dubious grounds that if staff in a particular project are provided with "sophisticated" equipment, other staff will demand the same. An additional difficulty in achieving the objective of spending the majority of their time away from the main office is the extent of paperwork all staff are required to complete. Hern comments, "the overwhelming expectation for compliance to the many specifics of standards of service ties overworked social workers to computers. Alone in an office with the door shut is not exactly describing the term social worker."

The neighbourhoods of these houses differ considerably. The Blanshard community centre is located in a low-income public housing project and in Warren's framework might be seen as a parochial community. The Burnside, Gorge, Tillicum house serves a low-income area marked by substandard housing and mobility of residents. It most closely resembles an anomic community. The communities of Fairfield and James Bay are located adjacent to the centre of the city and have a mixed population of both high- and low-income seniors, young families, and professionals. They might best be described as transitory. Another staff member was placed in the Native Indian Friendship Centre.

Victoria is well known in Canada as a tourist attraction and is the capital of the province. Three closely adjacent municipalities and the city constitute the Capital Regional District, which has responsibilities for certain functions such as water and regional planning and in turn these core municipalities are surrounded by no less than eight other municipalities. It is the second-largest urban area in the province with a total population of 325,000.

The project owes much to the experience and innovative ideas of its team leader, who is well known in the ministry for his strong convictions regarding a family-centred and community-responsive approach to child welfare. Regardless of the philosophy of the ministry—which has shifted from an almost exclusive focus on investigation to a family-centred approach and recently returned to investigation—Hern has consistently employed a community-centred approach in different offices and over a considerable period of time. The staff of the project have many years of experience in child welfare and are committed to this style of practice. Indeed, they view the project as an island of excellence within a ministry that, like many large organizations, has developed a plethora of cumbersome rules and regulations. When the B.C. Government Employees Union surveyed its members in the ministry about working conditions "over 1,200 members said loud and clear that the Ministry had failed on all counts—from consulting with workers and providing adequate resources and training to improving service delivery and enhancing the quality of service" (BCGEU, 1997: 1). This failing report card supported the conclusions of an earlier review by the Auditor General, which concluded that while the child welfare job is difficult, most of the morale and turnover problems were attributable to an organization that surrounded staff with regulations and was quick to assign blame but sparing in its rewards for work well done (Auditor General of B.C., 1992).

The Hazelton Office of the Ministry for Children and Families

In contrast to the southern, capital city of Victoria, Hazelton is a small northern community situated between the two larger towns of Smithers and Terrace. The Hazelton office serves a population of about 5,000 people scattered among three villages, seven First Nation bands, farms, and isolated homes. Although its topography differs substantially from Victoria, it, too, is a scenic place, with snow-covered mountains, deep valleys, and rushing rivers. Hazelton has a northern Canadian climate with temperatures often going to 30 degrees below zero, icy winds, and sufficient snow to discourage all but hardy northern residents. Those served by the Hazelton office are likely to be poor, to live in substandard housing, and—considering the numbers of First Nations people in the area—to be of Aboriginal descent.

If staff turnover is a problem throughout the ministry, nowhere is it felt more than in rural and remote offices in the north. The situation is so serious that the ministry recently offered a bonus to staff members who make a commitment to stay for three years. The reasons for the turnover are many and varied. Typically, new staff arrive in a new community to find a large and complicated workload crying for attention on the first day of work, an office where the most senior worker has been in place only a year or so and resources such as mental health services and homemaker and daycare programs that complement the child welfare job are in scarce supply. The ministry's recruitment efforts have traditionally targeted new graduates of Schools of Social Work across the country. Since most schools are located in southern cities, graduates seek employment in these urban areas. Many who move to northern communities are unused to the harsh climate and miss the leisure time and cultural activities so plentiful in larger communities. The work is exhausting, and if family or personal supports are not in place many a worker's response is to move to a vacant position in the south or to leave the ministry.

For the most part the Hazelton office has not experienced staff turnover of the kind typically found in the north. To be sure there has been a recurring problem of finding and keeping a supervisor, but for the most part staff have stayed, made a home in Hazelton, enjoy life in the north, and endorse the approach to practice that has developed over the years. Maurice Yee came to Hazelton from Vancouver, intending like many of his counterparts to stay for only a year. Thirteen years later he and his wife and children make their home in Hazelton and have no intentions of leaving. Greg Kormany also came from Vancouver, stayed for five years, and moved only because his wife entered nursing school at a college in the Kootenays. Tanya Buttress, a graduate of the School of Social Work at the University of Northern British Columbia, has been in Hazelton for five years. During my visit a worker on temporary assignment, and somewhat to the embarrassment of the permanent staff, described Hazelton as the "Camelot" of ministry offices, while not so effusive a former supervisor (who left only because his physician wife could not practise in Hazelton) was extremely positive about the commitment of staff to a community style of work.

Community Social Work in Victoria and Hazelton

Despite the differences in size and location of their respective communities, the approaches of the Victoria project and of the Hazelton office are very similar. The following discussion identifies the characteristics of their style of work and, where appropriate, points to differences between the two offices.

THE COMMUNITY MAKES THE OFFICE

One of the participants in the Hazelton interviews is a student in the decentralized Master of Social Work program of the University of Victoria. Cheryl Williams previously worked for a band council in the Hazelton area and is familiar with the approach of the Hazelton office. When asked for her views, Cheryl stated that "the community makes the office." The phrase sums up the commitment of Hazelton to be open to and learn from the surrounding communities. As noted above, the office serves a number of First Nation reserves and three villages, but the largest First Nation community of the Gitskan is well known for its kitchen-table style of decision-making. Decisions are made by gathering all affected together and discussing the issue until consensus is reached.

The Hazelton office has adopted the kitchen-table approach, which in many ways is similar to the family conferences initiated in New Zealand and now used in other jurisdictions (see, among other sources, Burford and Pennell, 1995; Maxwell and Morris, 1995). Thus, in responding to a situation of child neglect or abuse, Hazelton staff gather together all family members and concerned professionals such as band social workers and teachers. The discussion may last two to three hours and is not ended until everyone has agreed on the best plan for the child.

Being open to the community requires that child welfare staff leave the office and pay regular visits to schools, band council offices, and families. Being open means that staff are comfortable in the community and view it as a friendly place full of resources and helpful people. Community is also a place where privacy for the staff is limited by their commitment to live in the same area as their workplace. Staff have opted to have their phone numbers listed and they are accustomed to being called at home both by their "clients" and by professional colleagues like the RCMP. While occasionally resenting these at-home calls, staff recognize that it is the price to be paid for being part of a supportive community.

The staff in the Victoria project are also comfortable in the neighbourhood. They frequently encounter "clients" in the neighbourhood house and in nearby grocery stores. Like the Hazelton staff, they do not avoid such encounters but greet those they serve as they would their friends and professional colleagues.

While being strong supporters of the project, the directors and staff of neighbourhood houses have several concerns. In their view implementation of the vision has been flawed by the demands on child welfare staff for paper work and the time consumed by appearances in court. A particular complaint around implementation was the decision to assign one staff member to three neighbourhoods. While recognizing that this was brought about by the lack of staff, neighbourhood directors felt that such an inadequate arrangement was flirting with disaster since it is extremely difficult to become known and accepted in three different neighbourhoods.

A second issue is that some residents of one neighbourhood have become disturbed by the continuing presence of ministry staff, so much so that a member of the Board of Directors raised the matter at a board meeting. The board member reported that some of her friends have been reluctant to bring their children to the house because they fear that if the children behave badly in the presence of the ministry staff, this could be seen as poor parenting and a cause for an investigation. The board has taken this complaint seriously and will devote time to finding a resolution in the future. However, as the following discussion indicates, the issue can be dealt with by having ministry staff clarify their role and their approach to child welfare, and by demonstrating their approach on a day-to-day basis.

While acknowledging that the community-based approach has many positive features, a ministry concern has been voiced that neighbourhood houses may not be able to deal with very difficult parents and children. Such individuals may disrupt activities or behave in unacceptable ways and then be asked to leave the house. Yet neighbourhood house staff argue that they work with many individuals who exhibit behaviourial problems, and these are not just ministry clients. Again, where there is a relationship of mutual respect between staff of the neighbourhood house and the ministry, dealing with the occasional difficult individual is not an insurmountable problem.

SHOES ON OR OFF?

Greg Kormany, the staff member who left the Hazelton office, was nevertheless keen to participate in the interview and did so by phone. When asked to give his impressions of the Hazelton office Greg responded with the following anecdote.

> Together with a social work student I recently responded to a complaint of child neglect. On arriving at the house the man who answered the door invited us in, but asked that we take off our shoes. We complied with his request. Back at the office the student reported on the visit to the child protection consultant, who was most disturbed. He reminded us of the injunction stressed in in-service training that, when investigating a complaint, social workers should not remove their shoes.

The anecdote captures the sense of respect and courtesy shown to those they serve by staff in the Hazelton office and the Victoria project. The in-service training edict is based on the assumption that investigations are by definition intrusive and adversarial and that family members might act in a hostile or even violent fashion. Hence, social workers should be prepared for a quick exit and leaving one's shoes on readies one for this getaway. But the approach in Victoria and Hazelton is based a different assumption: that a first visit can begin with an offer of help and that taking shoes off, particularly when asked to do so, demonstrates respect and courtesy. Obviously, when the available information indicates that a child has been abused and particularly if there has been a pattern of violence, the investigation should proceed in the company of the police and with shoes on.

The values underpinning a "shoes off" stance are those of caring about people and respecting them. "The foundation of all best practice experiences was a trusted and respectful relationship, a genuine attachment between clients and workers within which problems and issues could be addressed in an authentic fashion" (Callahan et al., 1998: 13).

THE SAFETY OF CHILDREN

In B.C. and other provinces in Canada, child welfare agencies have devoted and are devoting enormous resources to the development and implementation of risk assessment instruments. The intent of these instruments is to ensure that children are protected from neglect and abuse. While no one would argue with this laudable objective, analyses of their ability to assess and predict these conditions have varied from mild to harsh criticism. Thus one comprehensive review concluded that "the best one can hope for at present is that the risk assessment model selected (and implemented) will be one more source of information that can provide some confirmatory evidence to supplement caseworkers' judgments" (Michalski, Alaggia, and Trocme, 1996: 18).

The fascination with and focus on risk assessment has effectively diverted attention from other ways of preventing the neglect and abuse of children. An alternative method of protecting children can be found in the Victoria project and in Hazelton. In these communities staff have a wide range of contacts and know the circumstances of many families. Just as Jane Jacobs argued many years ago that eyes on the street make for safer neighbourhoods, so too does the knowledge of staff and their network of contacts combine to keep children safe (Jacobs, 1963). The knowledge of staff is far deeper and more extensive than the information gained from the invasive approach of risk assessment. Gillian Mullins, a staff member in the Victoria project, illustrated this point with the following anecdote. In an initial interview a mother said, "my neighbour, who knows you, said I should not hold anything back, because you know everything that goes on around here." And the family conference style of decision-making in Hazelton allows the knowledge of family members and of professionals to be brought to the table. The final decision, then, is one made by all concerned and in a very real way provides support for child welfare staff.

BRINGING CHILDREN INTO CARE

It is apparent from the above that the Victoria project and the Hazelton office focus their efforts on keeping children in their own homes. They do this by providing support to parents in a variety of ways depending on the resources available to them. But such efforts are not always successful and on occasion children must be removed from parents and placed in the care of the state. Although Hazelton and Victoria are far from unique in preferring that such action occurs with the consent of parents, they are perhaps distinct in that their overall approach virtually requires consent. Indeed, Hazelton has achieved a remarkable record in this regard: in the past five years 125 children have been taken into care and in only two instances did the parents of these children contest the matter. Most of the children were in care on a voluntary arrangement for only a short period of time.

An irony of some moment should be noted here. In the past, bringing a child into care with parental consent required completing an agreement between the office and the parents. This approach not only avoided the time-consuming, expensive, and frequently adversarial process of court action but also secured the co-operation of parents in planning for the child's future. However, in B.C. voluntary agreements became so numerous and differed so considerably between ministry offices that a voluntary agreement review board was created to bring about some consistency in these agreements. The procedures established by the review board have become so extensive that some offices now view court action as a less cumbersome way of proceeding.

Evidence of Effectiveness

The child welfare enterprise has devoted limited time to measuring the effectiveness of its work. Several reasons are noted here. First the ever-increasing volume of work demands that resources be allocated to first-line work—the work of protecting children. Most child welfare agencies have not developed research units with the mandate to engage in longitudinal studies, and the differences among provinces on a number of variables makes the task of collecting national statistics extremely difficult. Second, the enterprise is plagued by uncertainty as to how to measure success. Does effective work mean that few children are taken into care, or does this suggest that inadequate attention is being paid to the investigation of complaints of child neglect and abuse? And if children are taken into care, when does the state as substitute parent claim success? When children are returned to their parents? When they are discharged from care at the age of 19? When these children become self-supporting adults? Third, all involved in child welfare move and move frequently. The mobility of families with young children, of teenage wards, of staff, and of foster parents makes the tracking of progress a challenge of no small order.

One measure that received attention in the past was the number of children in care. The rationale for this measure rested on the well-known difficulties experienced by the state as a substitute parent and on the enduring ties between parents and children in even the most dysfunctional of families. Thus, the lower the number of children in care the more successful the enterprise. But this measure did not take into account important factors such as the characteristics of the population being served and the adequacy of the procedures and resources established to ensure that children were safe. A complementary measure that has not received much attention would be to track how children are taken into care. The agreement of parents that care is necessary for a period of time creates a partnership between the state and the parents focussed on the interests of the child. Such a partnership paves the way for agreement for the future of the child whether this a return to the parental home, a shared-care arrangement, or long-term care by the state. If this measure is an indication of success, the Hazelton office has achieved a remarkable record.

KNOWLEDGE AND SKILLS TO DO THE WORK

It was noteworthy that in both of these case studies staff had difficulty articulating the kinds of knowledge and skills required for their approaches to practice. They began by identifying personal characteristics and values rather than knowledge acquired in either an academic setting or during in-service training. Characteristics such as honesty, being comfortable in situations where it is far from clear what should be done, the ability to juggle many tasks at the same time, the ability to confront parents, and, perhaps above all, genuinely liking and respecting people were consistently mentioned as the key attributes. In both offices, staff argued that the maturity that comes from having lived through varied life and job experiences, including raising children, was essential for effective work in child welfare. And in Hazelton it is clearly necessary to be at home in the north. The recreational pursuits of skiing, hiking, fishing, and hunting may not appeal to all but are intrinsic to the lifestyle of northern communities. In part the inability to identify specific skills and knowledge for community social work may be explained by noting the similarity of this role to the generic model of social work practice. The generic model embraces practice with individuals, groups, and communities and has been the dominant approach in the curricula of Schools of Social Work in recent years. The core skills identified by Lee (1999) for community organization—listening, information gathering, analysis, facilitation, and negotiation—are to be found in generic and community social work approaches.

The academic background of staff in both offices varies from master and bachelor degrees in social work to baccalaureates in a number of disciplines. And to the consternation of the writer, who has spent most of his career in Schools of Social Work, some staff with degrees in social work were hard-pressed to identify the contributions of these programs. When pushed, one stated that a course on northern social work practice had been helpful and added that a course on community work that included community analysis and information about cultural diversity would have been useful. Many staff pointed to the importance of analytical thinking, of being able to think through confusing situations both with "clients" and in supervisory sessions. A number of academic courses had assisted them to develop this skill.

Implications for Child Welfare

SEPARATING THE INVESTIGATION AND SUPPORT FUNCTIONS
One of the long-standing debates in child welfare is whether the investigative and support functions should be separated or combined into a single role. I have been among those who have argued strenuously that the two functions are incompatible (Wharf and Callahan, 1993; Lindsey and Hawkins, 1994). The argument holds that investigating complaints of neglect and abuse sets up such an adversarial relationship between the investigator and families that it is exceedingly difficult if not impossible to recast the relationship into one of support. I should add that my position on this issue has been anchored in Callahan's suggestion that neglect should be removed from legislation in child welfare, that abuse should be seen as a crime and assigned to the criminal justice system, and that the entire resources of the child welfare enterprise should be devoted to supporting families (Callahan, 1993). Needless to say, this radical notion has not been adopted by any child welfare juris-

diction in Canada and, indeed, most have clung to the tradition of combining the functions.

The first dent in my conviction that the functions should be divided came as a result of my participation in a study of best practice in child welfare in B.C. (Callahan et al., 1998). In this study those being served, workers, supervisors, and staff of voluntary agencies were asked to identify best practice. There was substantial agreement that best practice occurred when workers treated those being served with respect; included them in the formulation of the problems and in the planning to resolve these; and were frank, open, and consistent in providing information. In short, the study concluded that best practice meant a positive and trusting relationship between worker and those being served and that such relationships could occur in both the support and investigative functions.

The Hazelton experience is consistent with the best practice study. Unless there is evidence of violence in the home, when a police officer would accompany the worker, an initial visit in Hazelton is based on an offer of help—on a "shoes-off" approach—and this approach is continued throughout the rest of the contact with the family. The experience of the Hazelton office is that investigations can be carried out in a helpful, supportive fashion. When necessary, extended family members and other professionals are involved at an early stage to assist parents to recognize that the safety of the children must be their paramount concern.

Staff in the Victoria project are responsible for providing support services and monitoring the ongoing safety of children. However, when a situation appears to warrant an investigation, that function is assumed by a member of the investigation team. In most cases the investigator approaches and deals with the family in a very "professional," i.e., distant and objective, fashion. In some instances the positive relationship built up with families by project staff can be threatened if not drastically altered as a consequence of the investigation. The consequences of this changed relationship become very apparent when a child is apprehended and the family support staff are then required to resume the relationship. Taking children into care is a traumatic experience not only for the family but for the community and hence relationships can change not just for one family but for many. In short, if Victoria staff had their way, they would prefer to be responsible also for investigations.

CAN A "SHOES-OFF" APPROACH WORK IN OTHER COMMUNITIES?

One of the distinguishing characteristics of the Hazelton office is the way in which it has gradually adapted its approach to the kitchen style of decision-making found in its surrounding communities. The question raised now is, would a "shoes-off" approach work in other communities? A number of responses to the question argue for the affirmative. First, staff in the Victoria project have taken an almost identical approach and in a number of different neighbourhoods. Second, Greg Kormany reported that transplanting the Hazelton approach in his new community was relatively easy. Third, the approaches in both Hazelton and Victoria exemplify the characteristics of best practice identified in the study noted above. "Shoes off" seems to require the following ingredients:

- staff who like people, who are mature, and who preferably have experience in child welfare;

- staff who prefer to get out of the office and spend time in the community;

- staff who can accept a degree of uncertainty and ambivalence;

- a supervisor or senior worker who can provide leadership both by modelling this approach to practice and by "protecting" workers from the barrage of contradictory commands from the organization.

COMMUNITY-BASED AND COMMUNITY-RESPONSIVE PRACTICE

The concept of community social work accurately portrays the style of work adopted in the Victoria project and the Hazelton office. Community social work is based in and responsive to communities. In our view it is effective and appropriate and indeed may be a pragmatic and reasonable approach for offices of provincial ministries to adopt since it does not unduly disturb the status quo of ministry practice. Provincial ministries or departments of child welfare in Canada are very conservative organizations. They carry out the mandate to protect children by assessing the capacity of parents to care for their children. This narrow focus excludes attention to the environment of families, such as poverty, substandard housing, and unsafe neighbourhoods. The focus is supported by politicians of a neoconservative stance and by many senior managers and first-line staff[1] whose social work education and orientation have been dominated by a clinical approach to child welfare. Hence, for many child welfare agencies community work is virtually a foreign concept.

As noted in Chapter 1, a community-minded minister in B.C. initiated a community development branch, but while seen by many staff and by an external review to make valuable contributions, the branch was eliminated when a new minister and deputy were appointed (Swets, Rutman, and Wharf, 1995). As Chapters 4 and 5 demonstrate, agencies that enjoy a relative measure of independence from the state provide more promising auspices for community organizing than provincial ministries.

Nevertheless, in addition to being an appropriate approach in its own right, community social work can become a stepping stone to other organizing strategies. Two suggestions are noted here. First, the current composition of case management arrangements, whereby professional staff meet to discuss the situations of families, could be changed to include the individuals being served, as has occurred in the family-centred approach of the Hazelton office. It would not stretch imagination and energy too far to turn family conferences into social planning activities, to develop a community plan that ensured that services were connected and responsive to the needs of those being served. Indeed, as McKenzie notes in Chapter 5, West Region devotes considerable energy and resources to conducting annual plans that are determined by all who wish to participate.

Community social work can also pave the way to community control of programs. For example, a long-term objective of the Victoria project is to transfer some responsibilities and resources held by the ministry to neighbourhood houses. At the present time the ministry has established an intricate set of regulations and criteria that must be used to determine eligibility for programs such as daycare and respite care and homemaker services. Ironically, to establish eligibility for these programs staff and parents must define a family situation that claims, although the children are not at present in need of protection, that they might be in the future unless some support services are put into place. As one critic of the child welfare scene in the U.S. has pointed out, "in many states, a family's access to child welfare services is contingent on the parent's failure to pass the test of parental adequacy as administered by the very state agency charged with helping them" (Morris-Bilotti, 1991: 6). In other words, parents have to admit failure in order to get the services they need! Staff of the Victoria project argue that allocating block grants to neighbourhood houses would enable these centres to enhance their existing daycare programs and make them available to all neighbourhood residents without their having to apply through elaborate and demeaning eligibility procedures.

note

1. The term "first line" was coined by Professor Michael Prince in a class on Connecting Policy and Practice in a graduate program at the University of Victoria. The class discussion was focused on finding appropriate replacements for military language like "front line."

references

Auditor General of British Columbia. 1992. "Managing Professional Resources." Victoria, unpublished paper.

B.C. Government Employees Union. 1997. *Report Card on the Ministry for Children and Families*. Burnaby, B.C.

Burgess, J., R. Hern, and B. Wharf. 2000. "From Case and Client to Citizen: An Innovation in Child Welfare Practice," in M. Callahan and S. Hessle, eds., *Valuing the Field: Child Welfare in an International Context*. Aldershot, Hampshire: Ashgate Press.

Burford, G., and J. Pennell. 1995. "Family Group Decision Making: An Innovation in Child and Family Welfare," in J. Hudson and B. Galaway, eds., *Child Welfare in Canada, Research and Policy Implications*. Toronto: Thompson Educational Publishing.

Callahan, M., B. Field, C. Hubberstey, and B. Wharf. 1998. *Best Practice in Child Welfare*. Victoria: University of Victoria, School of Social Work.

Jacobs, J. 1961. *The Death and Life of Great American Cities*. New York: Random House.

Lee, B. 1999. *The Pragmatics of Community Organization*. Mississauga, ON: Common Act Press.

Lindsay, D., and W.E. Hawkins. 1994. "Should the Police Have Greater Authority in Investigating Cases of Suspected Child Abuse? Yes!," in E. Gambrill and T.J. Stein, eds., *Controversial Issues in Child Welfare*. Boston: Allyn and Bacon.

Maxwell, G.M., and A. Morris. 1995. "Deciding About Justice for Young People in New Zealand: The Involvement of Families, Victims and Culture," in J. Hudson. and B. Galaway, eds., *Child Welfare in Canada, Research and Policy Implications*. Toronto: Thompson Educational Publishing.

Michalski, J.H., R. Alaggia, and N. Trocme. 1996. *A Literature Review of Risk Assessment Models*. Centre for Applied Social Research, Faculty of Social Work, University of Toronto.

Morris-Billotti, S. 1991. "Is an Integrated, Child Centred, Family Focused, Community Based

Prevention System Possible?" Illinois: State Department of Children and Family Services, unpublished paper.

Swets, R., D. Rutman, and B. Wharf. 1995. *The Community Development Initiative of the Ministry of Social Services*. Victoria: Child, Family and Community Research Program, School of Social Work, University of Victoria.

Wharf, B., and M. Callahan. 1993. "The Case for Removing Child Abuse and Neglect Investigations from the Mandate of Child Welfare," in L. Bella, P. Rowe, and D. Costello, eds., *Rethinking Social Welfare: People, Policy and Practice*. St. John's, Nfld.

part two ————————————————————————————

COMMUNITY CHILD WELFARE: EXAMPLES FROM QUEBEC

LINDA DAVIES, KAREN FOX, JULIA KRANE & ERIC SHRAGGE

Introduction

In the last two decades, the child welfare system has undergone a series of dramatic changes. Broadly speaking, child welfare services have moved from concern for the social welfare of children and their families to a more restricted concern with detecting and investigating instances of child abuse and neglect (Howe, 1992). Escalating reports of suspected abuse and neglect, higher caseloads, shrinking resources and lack of support both for families and for workers have all contributed to the narrowing of the focus of contemporary child welfare to one more aptly characterized as child protection (English and Pecora, 1994; Parton, Thorpe, and Wattam, 1997; Wharf, 1993). Recently, child welfare practice has come under sustained criticism concerning its preoccupation with detection of high risk cases and its adversarial relations with clients (Buckley, 2000; de Montigny, 1995; McMahon, 1998; Parton, Thorpe, and Wattam, 1997; Wharf, 1993). This preoccupation with risk has distorted the distribution of available resources of both time and money. Parton et al. (1997), for example, note that efforts to detect child-abusing families have led to agencies being overwhelmed by an explosion of referrals, the majority of which are not sustained but rather filtered out of the system. Thus, while these agencies may experience a great deal of organizational activity in the form of investigations and case conferences, little social work support is, in the end, actually provided to families (ibid., 1997).

Feminist analysts, in particular, have drawn attention to the gendered nature of child welfare, its workforce, client population, and the assumptions underlying intervention. They have suggested that the state mandate to ensure the protection of children is in reality a process of evaluating maternal capacity without providing much support. A growing feminist literature on mothering has challenged the unrealistic expectations placed on women to silently cope despite inadequate material and emotional resources. They have drawn attention to the denigration of mothers whose children are found wanting and have documented how mother blame is endemic in the "helping professions" (Caplan and McCorquodale, 1985; Carter, 1999; Krane, 1997; Swift, 1995). Feminists have argued that the discourse of maternal sacrifice and the accompanying invisibility of the actual labour and resources necessary to accomplish mother work tend to reinforce a binary division between good and bad mothers in child welfare assessments (Carter, 1999; Davies and Krane, 1996; Krane, 1997; Krane and Davies, 2000; Swift, 1995). Distrust between social workers and their clients and alienation of mothers from the child welfare system often result. It is in this climate that the community sector of social work has become increasingly active.

The chapter explores this trend through an examination of two organizations that aim to support mothers in the community. Like child welfare clients, these mothers are disproportionately poor, young, immigrant, from visible minorities, and single. Under the rubric of supportive services to families, we suggest that the voluntary community sector is an important yet undervalued sector of child welfare activity. As a backdrop for understanding the case studies, we describe the evolution of the community movement in Quebec from the 1960s to the present. We then present a more detailed description of the CLSCs— the networks of comprehensive health and social service organizations that exist across the province. Though CLSCs work in partnership with the Department of Youth Protection to pursue the welfare of children, mandated youth protection functions clearly rest with the latter state institution. Next, we offer a brief overview of the legislative context for child welfare practice in Quebec. Following our case studies, we discuss the implications for the development of a community-based orientation for child welfare.

Community Movement: From Organizing and Advocacy to State Partnerships

Since the 1960s, the community movement in Quebec has undergone significant changes. Analysts have identified three distinct periods in the evolution of the community movement (Panet-Raymond and Mayer, 1997; Shragge, 1999; Shragge and Fontan, 2000) marked by shifts in the nature and extent of practices, programs, and services, as well as changing relationships between community-based organizations and formal state institutions.

In the 1960s and 1970s, the community sector moved from its origins as an extension of churches and voluntary organizations to a grassroots movement. This was a period of rapid social reform with growth and secularization of health and social services. Community organizations and groups, acting locally, mobilized citizens to put in place new types of services and projects. In addition, they challenged policy directions at all levels and denounced those holding corporate power. These new forms of action shared a common commitment to local participation and democracy. Challenges to social service professionals were common. Activists were optimistic about the potential of community action as a vehicle for social change. Further, in the context of burgeoning state programs and financial support for innovative experiments, community organizations were well situated to expand their activities. Community activists and service providers engaged in common struggles. For example, a welfare rights group in Pointe-St-Charles in Montreal collaborated with a local clinic on a campaign to use welfare regulations regarding malnutrition to force an increase in welfare benefits. This example illustrates joint efforts by service and action organizations to challenge government policies and agencies and secure funds to aid in their cause.

As Keck and Fulks (1997) noted, this decade was one in which funds were available for a variety of community-based projects. Service groups, such as community clinics, challenged the role of professionals and demanded their direct accountability to citizens' committees. They trained local residents to carry out service provision functions. They created democratic opportunities for the expression of local citizens to manage their projects. In this period of social reform, the experiments launched by community organizations became models for the expanding social and health services. Notably, community clinics created in working-class neighbourhoods were copied on a large-scale by the provincial government in the form of CLSCs, community-based health and social service centres. At first glance similar to community clinics, the CLSCs differed on a number of significant counts. They were controlled through provincial structures and funding processes. They were not accountable to the local community. Growing professionalization and bureaucratic structures quickly made it clear that services were not to be mixed with radical politics. CLSCs, as it turns out, have become central in the provision of service as well as in the organization of new local services.

From the late 1970s and into the 1980s, attacks on the welfare state increased and there was a concomitant weakening of the political base of community organizations. In this period, along with a reduction in an action orientation, there was a rapid expansion and growth of community service organizations (Hamel and Léonard, 1980). Some organizations were affiliated with emerging social movements, such as the women's movement, and brought important innovations and services such as shelters and rape crisis centres. These organizations upheld the democratic traditions of the previous period, maintained autonomy and negotiated directly with government through sectoral coalitions or "regroupements." Others, although locally organized, were more traditional. They limited citizen participation to governing boards and professionals played leadership roles. Government policies that regulated funding of community organizations promoted partnership between CLSCs and community-based services. These became the norm, and guided the emergence of new practices in areas such as services to youth and the elderly (Panet-Raymond, 1992). During these decades, community-based services became increasingly professionalized and began to specialize in specific service activities. They also lost their engagement with social change activities and community mobilization.

From 1990 to the present time, relations between the community sector and the government took new shape. Economic restructuring and globalization brought the highest levels of unemployment in the postwar period, particularly for young workers and women; blue-collar workers also were affected. Coupled with ongoing cuts in funding to social programs, community organizations were faced with severe social problems and reduced resources. New approaches were born and reborn out of necessity. Food banks and collective kitchens proliferated, and new community economic development (CED) organizations were created. These CED organizations marked a departure from previous traditions. They entered into partnership with trade unions, the private sector, and government, creating new organizations that supported local economic development and that worked with people excluded from the labour market in order to reduce unemployment.

More important for this discussion was the increased governmental recognition of the role and importance of community organizations. This was expressed through a variety of formal partnerships, involvement of the community sector in major economic summits, and the development of a "social economy" (Shragge and Fontan, 2000). In addition, the administration of social programs was transferred to regions. Among the consequences are that community organizations find themselves tied to a variety of decentralized regional bodies and negotiate funding through these administrations. These relationships are central in determining whether or not organizations receive support from the provincial government. The community sector has thus been pushed in a service direction that is complimentary to state agencies. At the same time, however, the community sector is able to offer flexible services from staff that are typically neither unionized nor permanent. One of the key organizations that has been central to managing and promoting the role of community organizations as local services providers has been the CLSC.

CLSCs: State Organizations in the Community

In 1993, the Ministry of Health and Social Services reorganized social services across the province. Up until this time, government social services agencies (Centre des Services Sociaux, CSS) held a broad mandate to provide both voluntary and court-ordered services to families. These social service centres, while retaining a child welfare mandate, were also responsible for providing social services for young adults and the elderly. They operated a separate department for their clientele requesting voluntary services and determined the type of preventive intervention directed toward families. A department of youth protection, legislated within each social service centre since 1979, held a restricted mandate to investigate and enforce court-ordered and contractual services for families whose children were found to be at risk under the law.

The reform in social services eliminated the voluntary mandate of the existing social service centres and replaced it with a legal one focused solely upon the application of the youth protection law. The social service agencies were reconstituted into Child and Youth Protection Centres (CYPC), overseen by the legislative mandate of the Youth Protection Act. Local communities, through their networks of the CLSCs, schools, and community organizations took on greater responsibility for the development of programs that reflected the concerns and needs of children and families living in poverty. The mandate of the Child and Youth Protection Centres was limited to those situations under investigation for abuse and neglect and for youth charged with offences under the Young Offenders Act.

The mandate of the CLSCs was expanded to provide all voluntary services. The 1993 reform established special teams in the CLSCs according to ages of children and intervention was directed to specific populations at risk, i.e., those under five years of age, school-aged, or in the adolescent years. In essence, CLSCs were expected to work in partnership with community organizations and the Child and Youth Protection Centres in an effort to provide a range of services for families at risk (Quebec, Minister of Health and Social Services, 1999a).

To elaborate, CLSCs are a network of comprehensive health and social service organizations across Quebec. As stated in the Act Respecting Health Services and Social Services (LQ, 1991: Chapter 42, art. 80, cited in Annual Report CLSC CDN: 8), the official mandate of the CLSC "is to offer, at the primary level of care, basic health and social services of a preventive or curative nature, and rehabilitation or reintegration services to the population of the territory served by it."

As noted previously, CLSCs were established during the reforms of the early 1970s and expanded to all areas of the province. Each CLSC has its own board of directors, with a small proportion elected from the locality. These organizations are accountable to the provincial government rather than local residents or staff. CLSCs are not considered community organizations per se. Rather, they represent governmental structures with flexibility to respond to local conditions. To provide a generic overview of a typical CLSC is near impossible. With the exception of recognizing that their structures are bureaucratic and their staff is unionized, dramatic variations exist across the network of CLSCs. Briefly, some CLSCs provide medical services as their primary function; others specialize in services to the elderly, and still others focus on young families. Some have several hundred employees including medical doctors, nurses, social workers, psychologists, physiotherapists, and occupational therapists and a variety of home-care workers. Others have a limited staff. Community organizers are employed in some CLSCs, and have a provincial-wide organization. Their roles vary but many of them are involved in initiating and supporting the development of community services and building partnerships between organizations at the local level. They are particularly central to defining the type of service or activity that the CLSC will support. It should be noted that some provincial bodies insist on the support of the CLSC before they agree to fund grass-roots organizations.

Since their founding, CLSCs have undergone a number of reforms. Most notably, CLSCs absorbed non-statutory social work functions. Prior to this reform, many of these services were integrated with statutory services. Social workers in CLSCs do not have the legal power to compel a family to seek and secure help. The provision of services by CLSC is "voluntary," and their service emphasis is placed on "prevention." The nature of CLSC services to families and children at risk thus stand in stark contrast to the functions, responsibilities, and nature of services offered by the Child and Youth Protection Centres.

Child Welfare: State vs. Community Intervention

Child welfare in Canada is recognized through statutory laws that establish the extent of, and limits to, state intervention in families. Child-welfare practitioners are authorized to investigate, assess, intervene and protect only when parental care has fallen below a certain standard. Canadian child welfare services are thus residual in nature, based on a norm of non-interference (Bala, 1991; Corby, 1997). A major preoccupation of child welfare has been articulating the conditions and procedures that warrant state intrusion into private family life (Krane, 1997). Through statutory laws based on such principles as meeting children's best interests, offering service with the least intrusion, and supporting family autonomy, the state becomes involved in the private sphere of families only when absolutely necessary to ensure the protection of children at great risk of abuse or neglect. Quebec is no exception. In 1977, the government of Quebec centralized the application of youth protection services with the adoption of the current youth protection law. The Youth Protection Act, enforced in 1979, represented a major shift in the debate between children's rights and parental authority and the rightful responsibility of the state to determine matters of youth protection. Briefly, the Youth Protection Act, applied to persons under the age of 18 years, delineates the conditions through which the security and/or development of children would be understood to be at risk, as well as the conditions of mandatory reporting by professionals.

Central to youth protection legislation in this province has been the notion of parental authority. As with other provinces, Quebec's Youth Protection Act has upheld the belief that parents' rights and ultimate responsibility to provide care for their children may only be mediated by the state in circumstances of predefined risk. However, Quebec youth protection law delineates several avenues by which parental authority will be maintained and respected. The first focuses upon the development of an intervention plan directed towards finding a solution to the protection problems that brought the child and her/his family before the department of youth protection. The second principle stipulates that every effort must be made to maintain the child in her/his family environment. If this is impossible, the intervention plan must pursue options to promote the return of children to their families.

Quebec's Child and Youth Protection Centres focus on cases after risk is identified rather than on the prevention of risk in the first instance. Moreover, given the context of contemporary child welfare practice alluded to earlier, CYPC workers face difficult and complex cases involving circumstances such as substance abuse and domestic violence. At the same time, these workers have insufficient time to offer support and locate resources for the families they serve. It is thus not surprising that prevention and voluntary components of service are delegated to CLSCs and the voluntary community sector. Community support, it is thought, might alleviate many stresses experienced by families with children at potential risk. Though the benefits of access to social support through community agencies has been noted by researchers in the field (Cameron, 1995), the potential of the community sector in protection activities per se has received minimal attention to date (Davies, McKinnon, Rains, and Mastronardi, 1999). In the next sections, we examine the activities and functions of two organizations that are implicated, albeit ambivalently, in the protection and well-being of children.

CLSC Côte-des-Neiges: Support and Prevention in the Welfare of Children

The CLSC Côte-des-Neiges serves a large and diverse community with a population of 126,665. Its population includes high concentrations of poverty with pockets of affluence and high levels of recent immigration.[1] In the district of Côte-des-Neiges itself, 47.1 per cent of residents were born outside of Canada; in Snowdon, the figure is 54.7 per cent. In the catchment area of the CLSC Côte-des-Neiges, the mother tongue of over 40 per cent of residents is neither English nor French. Single parents head over 30 per cent of families. Using Statistics Canada measures of poverty, the rate is 38.4 per cent in Côte-des-Neiges and 42.3 per cent in Snowdon. Poverty is highly concentrated among those below 17 years of age and in families headed by single mothers. The unemployment rate for men is around 18 per cent and for women around 15 per cent.

The CLSC Côte-des-Neiges has attempted to fashion programs that take poverty and marginalization into account, and to reach families before major problems arise. Although not mandated to engage in child protection, this CLSC contributes to the well-being of children and families through its regular schedule of services and its more experimental programs. Our analysis draws on information derived from the 1999-2000 Annual Report of the CLSC Côte-des-Neiges, and an in-depth interview with a social worker who has been employed there for several years and involved in the outreach project. In addition, one of the co-authors has worked on the boards and organizing committees in that community alongside of CLSC community organizers.

Similarly, our understandings of the second organization we discuss, the Groupe des Jeunes Meres (GJM), derives from the participation of one of the authors with the organization in a variety of capacities including program development and membership on the board of directors. For this chapter, we conducted an in-depth interview with the agency's co-ordinator.

The CLSC describes itself as a comprehensive health program that "brings together under one roof the priorities, concerns, and the objectives of the Family and Child Health, Youth Health, Clinical Services and Refugee Assistance programs" (Annual Report: 14). It is committed to an "inter-establishment dialogue"(ibid.: 15). The divisions of mandate imposed by the provincial government are explicit, but at the same time, the organization recognizes the importance of creating mechanisms for working together along the lines of "continuity in the dispensation of services" (ibid.: 14). The CLSC defines five program areas: social adaptation, physical health, public health, mental health, and social integration. Social adaptation and physical health programs have the potential to aid in the welfare of children at the community level. For example, the CLSC works with pregnant women before and after the births of their children. Specific programs are aimed at maternal and infant care, including prenatal and postnatal classes and visits, and a variety of medical services for babies and children including nutrition supplement of eggs, milk, and oranges. The organization also offers a program that provides a homemaker or other assistance when a parent needs respite and relief. These services have the potential to prevent problems through early detection and intervention.

Programming under the rubric of social adaptation aims "to reduce the number of cases of sexual abuse, violence, and negligence toward children and young people, and mitigate the consequences of these problems" (ibid.: 15). Prevention of wife abuse, programs to assist violent spouses, and work aimed at developing parenting capacities are social service priorities and come in the forms of individual, group, and family services. Other programs include stimulation activities for children, parental support activities, a mutual assistance group for parents, and a drop-in daycare centre for mothers to address personal issues such as self-esteem, violence, and anger.

As can be seen, the CLSC offers a comprehensive range of services targeted to a voluntary clientele. The CLSC mandate stands in stark contrast to the Child and Youth Protection Centre's formal statutory mandate to work with families where children are deemed at risk according to Youth Protection Law. Although supposedly a clear division exists, the practice reality indicates far more overlap between these two government agencies. Generally speaking, the same families may receive services from both institutions at different points in time, but not services from both institutions simultaneously. If a CLSC worker is involved and the case is reported to the CYPC, s/he withdraws service in favour of the youth protection worker. If the case is closed by the CYPC, the family must again turn to the CLSC for service. Because the Child and Youth Protection Centre is inundated with reports that merit investigation, and often operates with waiting lists based on a hierarchy of risk categories, increasingly difficult cases enter into the CLSC system. Thus, the clear distinction between the CYPC and the voluntary nature of CLSC services is murky in practical terms. A case example, offered during our interview with a seasoned CLSC worker, illustrates typical difficulties and tensions in CLSC child welfare practice.

A father came to the CLSC for help. He and his wife are immigrants. Along with their eight children, they are living in a two-bedroom apartment. He reported that his 13-year-old daughter was acting out. He described her as being out of control. Neither parent could enforce discipline, and the teen ran away from home. The social worker requested police assistance to find the girl and return her to the home. The parents insisted they could no longer cope with the girl. They feared that their jobs were jeopardized due to absences from dealing with their daughter. In response, the CLSC worker contacted the CYPC for help. This was not the first call to the protection centre. In fact, this child had been placed previously after the CLSC social worker pressured the CYPC to take the case. At that time, the child remained in placement for one month and was then returned home, at which point the Child and Youth Protection Centre withdrew involvement. On this occasion, the CYPC was reluctant to reactivate the case, arguing that it was not urgent enough to warrant their involvement and thus no services or resources would be forthcoming. As a result, the CLSC worker faced clients who were demanding temporary placement for their child. The CLSC could not deliver this resource; removal and placement of children are not within their mandate. According to the CLSC social worker, "everyone passed it on." Cases like this one fall between the cracks, and ultimately few involved come away satisfied. Increasingly heavy demands on CYPC workers and fewer resources result in their offloading lower risk cases to the CLSC, which in turn results in a detraction of CLSC preventive functions.

The CLSC also reached out to sectors of its catchment area in which residents are most isolated. The Mountain Sights Project exemplifies an innovative preventive child welfare initiative. This project began in the early 1990s. It was established to reach out to immigrants from South Asia and Southeast Asia who were not using the services of the CLSC. Social workers and community workers went door-to-door to introduce themselves. They rented a small apartment on the street in an effort to bring CLSC services closer to the people. From this space, a nurse worked with pregnant women, focusing on nutrition. Concerned about premature delivery and low birth weight, the outreach aimed at assisting the women before and after childbirth. A social worker set up an after-school program to assist children with their studies. This program seemed particularly necessary for immigrant children to help them succeed and integrate better in schools where the language of instruction was French. A Café Rencontre was organized as a meeting place for informal gathering and socializing. Here the social worker started a group for adolescents in the area. Accessing funds from the government, a drug prevention program was launched for youths between the ages of 11 and 18 years. The community worker facilitated role plays and organized discussion groups on topics such as violence, family relations, drugs, drinking, sexuality; she also involved several youth in producing a video on these topics. The program was so successful that the youths continued to meet for nearly three years. Despite its success, the program was terminated because of internal conflicts within the CLSC, which resulted in the community worker leaving and no one else being prepared to continue the work.

La Groupe des Jeunes Mères: A Community-Based Organization of Young Mothers

The Groupe des Jeunes Mères (GJM) offers a case illustration that enables us to explore the contradictions in the current government notion of "community as partner" in child welfare. Located in Pointe St. Charles, a working-class neighbourhood in Montreal, the GJM was begun as a pilot project in 1987. Community workers from the Pointe St. Charles Community Clinic[2] started this group for young mothers, most of who were not involved with community organizations in the area. The philosophy of the Pointe Clinic, at that time, was based on a class analysis that attempted to link the development of services and community programs to the wider structural issues of poverty as experienced by the residents of that neighbourhood. The Pointe Clinic supported an ongoing process of community organizing and the development of new local initiatives. All of the women involved with the GJM had

been receiving services at the Pointe Clinic. The Clinic helped support the GJM initiative through the provision of a babysitting program
for the mothers and transportation to and from the Pointe Clinic. As
well, it organized training for the childcare program.

GJM emphasized a self-help group approach. The mothers themselves determined the type of service they wanted to provide and developed links with other community organizations. They developed links
with welfare rights and housing organizations. During the first several
years, many of the women were able to obtain co-operative housing
and became involved with community advocacy groups. The solid
connection between the Pointe Clinic and GJM reinforced the establishment of an independent community organization of mothers. GJM,
while providing services to children and mothers, was at the same time
able to set its own agenda and vision for the organization.

In 1990, GJM was incorporated as a community organization, thus
becoming officially autonomous from the Clinic. The organization now
defines itself as a family centre. At present, it has a Board of Directors
comprised of seven people: five mothers, the co-ordinator, and one
worker. There are 12 employees. These changes took place over a period
of several years. Similarly, over time, the needs of a core group of mothers and their children were changing as they became older. These older
mothers became involved in program planning. With the active participation of 40 members, a range of programs was created: an early
learning/child stimulation program, a group program for children up
to 12 years of age, an adolescent mother support program, a toy lend-
ing library, and weekly discussion groups, which continue to provide
the basis for program planning and reaching other young mothers.

GJM has developed a strong community network and is committed
to the principles of citizen participation. Despite this autonomy, the
organization also faces ongoing tension with government because of
the latter's notions of "the community as partner." All CLSCs receive
a directive, determined by the Ministry of Health and Social Services,
to provide services to children at risk in their catchment areas. They
are dependent upon organizations, such as GJM, to address the service
needs of these families. At the same time, CLSCs hold community groups
accountable to them as a condition for the support provided. Tension
emerges as groups try to assert their autonomy within the partnership
relation structured between government, CLSCs, (or in this case the
Pointe Clinic), and community groups. In her interview, the GJM co-
ordinator provided an example of these tensions arising from varying
conceptions of young mothers vis-à-vis their relationship—clients or

participants with the organization. She recalled a debate with another community worker:

> Well in your community group, who comes—is it a client, participant, or member? Because lots of groups have clients in their organizations and even me, I have people who come in and say, "the clients." And I say, "well, here, they are 'participants,'" and they are fine with that because they agree with the mission. It is a switch [in] mentality—I mean their feelings are in the right place, you just have to change their vocabulary. But some people see "clients" coming to community groups.

This negotiation of definitions illustrates some of the difficulties for women in these community organizations as they attempt to maintain an autonomous vision. The debate reflects tendencies in the community movement as a whole. Professionalization of many of these groups has grown, accompanied by a service ideology. In contrast, GJM adheres to a membership model with democratic participation reflecting a strong tradition within that community.

Another tension also confronted by these types of community organizations is derived from assumptions made by funding agencies about proper maternal care of children. Funding bodies set criteria; as a result, the CLSCs/Pointe Clinic face pressures to have community groups comply with service assumptions. Thus, while the Clinic that started GJM remains committed to the organization, their increased focus on service goals has led to confusion over how it should support an autonomous community group in a partnership relation. A clear example is seen in conflict around how to best approach adolescent pregnancy. The co-ordinator explains:

> Sometimes there's a nurse [from the Pointe Clinic] who feels being pregnant as a teenager should not exist, so you know, we are talking about workers and their values…. So then we say to them, "How do we make a link? How are you going to refer this young mother? Who is going to take care of this teenager in a way that is going to be positive? Who is going to support her in making a decision?" … They say, "Well, we're not sure what our priorities are, if it's prevention of pregnancy or working with teenage moth-

ers." I say, "Well, when you decide, you let us know." Meanwhile, she is pregnant; what do you do for her?

The distinction between the GJM vision and the services provided by the Pointe Clinic is not consistent, and there is no consultation between them on these issues. Ideas concerning appropriate maternal behaviour, addressing "problematic" maternal behaviour and government policy to identify populations at risk are central in the struggles faced by GJM in securing funding on their own terms. As the co-ordinator put it,

> When ... you want the money, you have to bring out all this [child] negligence, the difficulty they [mothers] have in taking care of their children, all these attachment problems. Then the whole [GJM] program becomes evaluated on these criteria. The funding bodies want to focus on risk ... so, for example, the focus of the group may become mothers and underweight babies rather than saying the mandate is mothers and babies. The mandate becomes "How are we going to stop small weight babies?"

The organization faces the dilemma of trying to access funds without pathologizing its clientele. To secure funding it uses a broad definition of risk despite increasing pressures to focus more narrowly upon services that are targeted for "at risk" families. GJM tries to maintain its autonomy and organize a program in which young mothers have a collective voice in defining their needs and shaping support programs.

Conclusion

The (Côtes-des-Neiges) Mountain Sights outreach project of the CLSC and the Groupe de Jeunes Mères represents an alternative approach to families needing support in caring for their children. Their services are based on a philosophy that views assistance for isolated mothers and families in difficulty as normal rather than a pathological instance of maternal failure. This stands in contrast to the dominant framework in child welfare where mothering work is often invisible and is based on the assumption that normal mothers ought to be able to cope with the daily demands of raising their children regardless of their access to support and resources. In contrast, the kinds of services described here are based on an explicit recognition of mothering work and the context in which the care of children take place. At the Mountain Sights outreach project and GJM, services to individuals and families were based on notions of support and mutual aid within their communities. The GJM extends this notion of community support in a particular way; the group tries to create equable relationships of solidarity between participants and staff and promote democratic decision-making.

The restricted mandate of the Child and Youth Protection Centres, brought about by the last reform, produced new ground for alternative approaches. These practices have to be situated within the history of community organizations and the wider community movement described above. As we argued earlier, this movement began as an autonomous protest movement, but over the years it has oriented its practices to the provision of service. These services, while innovative and oriented towards support, have become more professionalized. Further, in order to receive money from provincial departments, they have to establish partnership relations with the local CLSCs. While this process was taking place there were cutbacks to government services, and the void has been filled in many instances by community organizations. The situation becomes complex as their traditions come more directly into contact with the demands of government for service provision, and accountability for its delivery. As a consequence Panet-Raymond and Mayer (1997: 51) argue "community groups have taken on a strategy of critical co-operation or co-operative conflict in their partnership with the public sector."

The examples we described in the paper suggest that direct control by the CLSC—the Mountain Sights project—limited practice to a professional-controlled service. The Mountain Sights outreach program attempted by the CLSC, although effective in providing services in its neighbourhood, was unable to create a locally controlled organization that could sustain itself. The very existence of the project depended on the willingness of the CLSC to provide staff time. There was no direct accountability either to the residents or to those who used the services. The CLSC, as a professionalized state structure, did not move beyond a client-service model. On the other hand, GJM provides us with an example of co-operative conflict. It had established itself as more than a service, and had some power of self-definition. This is a crucial element and is more typical of Quebec's community organizations. There is ongoing pressure from the external partners, but at the same time an attempt is made to remain consistent with their original values and democratic traditions.

How has GJM been effective in protecting its autonomy? One contributing factor has been its ability to publicly articulate and clearly define its vision. From that position, the organization can enter into partnership, but with a strong view of why it is doing so and of the benefits and the risks involved. Further, the group has strong leadership from staff and the board, supportive networks with similar community groups, and traditions of autonomy and opposition derived from their communities. GJM is located in a neighbourhood that has a long tradition of opposition to government from local organization. It participates in a local coalition that advocates for changes in government policies and through this type of collective action the autonomy of the individual group is enhanced. These kinds of coalitions or "tables" are the means that service groups have used in Quebec to keep the social action tradition alive (Panet-Raymond and Mayer, 1997). The GJM has created a progressive and innovative practice for young mothers while successfully resisting pressures to move in the direction of a more traditional service.

Despite the success achieved by groups like GJM, maintaining this stance is growing more difficult. The Quebec government is attempting to rationalize its policies and funding for the community sector, and make recognition and subsequently funding contingent upon becoming a subcontracted service provider for the state (Quebec, 1999b). This danger is not new but is part of a gradual change in the relationship between the provincial government and community organizations. However, as White (1991: 81) argues, "the government of Quebec is harnessing community action to its own cause, but the independent voice of community action has never completely disappeared." For organizations like GJM, the provision of services through a democratic process with autonomy will continue if they are able to be part of a wider community-based movement that will work together and struggle for these values and practices. The challenge for community organizations is to offer needed support to families, while building sound democratic structures with active citizen involvement as a means to protect their integrity and autonomy. In addition, their oppositional stance and vision must be safeguarded. Consistent with feminism, these services recognize the capacity of people to build their own democratic organizations for support and solidarity.

notes

1. The CLSC serves two distinct neighbourhoods in the City of Montreal: Côtes-des-Neiges and Snowdon. In addition, it serves the two independent municipalities of Outremont and Town of Mount Royal.

2. The Pointe St. Charles community clinic plays a similar role and provides similar services to that of a CLSC. Its establishment pre-dates that of CLSCs and it has been able to retain an autonomous status as a community clinic, accountable directly to local residents but with the budget necessary to carry out the programs of a CLSC.

references

Bala, N. 1991. "An Introduction to Child Protection Problems," in N. Bala, J.P. Hornick, and R. Vogl, eds., *Canadian Child Welfare Law*. Toronto: Thompson Educational Publishing.

Buckley, H. 2000. "Child Protection: An Unreflective Practice," *Social Work Education* 19,3: 253-64.

Cameron, C. 1995. "The Nature and Effectiveness of Parent Mutual Aid Organizations in Child Welfare," in J. Hudson and B. Galaway, eds., *Child Welfare in Canada: Research and Policy Implications*. Toronto: Thompson, 66-81.

Caplan, P., and I. Hall-McCorquodale. 1985. "Mother Blaming in Major Clinical Journals," *American Journal of Orthopsychiatry* 55,3: 345-53.

Carter, B. 1999. *Who's to Blame: Child Sexual Abuse and Non-Offending Mothers*. Toronto: University of Toronto Press.

Corby, B. 1997. "Risk Assessment in Child Protection Work," in H. Kemshall and J. Pritchard, eds., *Good Practice in Risk Assessment and Risk Management*. London: Jessica Kingsley Publishers, 13-20

Côte-des-Neiges. 1999-2000. *Annual Report*.

Davies, L., and J. Krane. 1996. "Shaking the Legacy of Mother Blaming: No Easy Task for Child Welfare," *Journal of Progressive Human Services* 7,2: 3-22.

Davies, L., M. McKinnon, P. Rains, and L. Mastronardi. 1999. "Rethinking Child Protection Practice: Lessons from a Voluntary Service Agency. *Canadian Social Work Review*, 16,1: 103-16.

de Montigny, G. 1995. *Social Working: An Ethnography of Front-Line Practice*. Toronto: University of Toronto Press.

English, D., and P. Pecora. 1994. "Risk Assessment as a Practice Method in Child Protective Services," *Child Welfare* LXXIII,5: 451-73.

Hamel P., and J. Léonard. 1980. "Ambivalence des luttes urbain et ambiguité des intervention de l'état," *Revue internationale d'actioncommunautaire* 4,44: 74-82.

Howe, D. 1992. "Child Abuse and the Bureaucratisation of Social Work," *Sociological Review* 40,3: 490-508.

Keck, J., and W. Fulks. 1997. "Meaningful Work and Community Betterment: The Case of Opportunity for Youth and Local Initiatives Program, 1971-1973," in B. Wharf and M. Clague, eds., *Community Organizing: Canadian Experiences.* Toronto: Oxford University Press, 113-36.

Krane, J. 1997. "Least Disruptive and Intrusive Course of Action for Whom? Insights from Feminist Analysis of Practice in Cases of Child Sexual Abuse," in J. Pulkingham and G. Ternowetsky, eds., *Child and Family Policies.* Halifax: Fernwood Publishing.

Krane, J., and L. Davies. 2000. "Mothering and Child Protection Practice: Rethinking Risk Assessment," *Child and Family Social Work* 5,1: 35-45.

McMahon, A. 1998. *Damned If You Do, Damned If You Don't.* Aldershot, Hampshire: Ashgate Press.

Panet-Raymond, J. 1987. "Community Groups in Québec: From Radical Action to Voluntarism for the State," *Community Development Journal* 22,4: 281-86.

——. 1992. "Partnership: Myth or Reality?," *Community Development Journal* 27,2: 156-65.

——. and R. Mayer. 1997. "The History of Community Development in Quebec," in B. Wharf and M. Clague, eds., *Community Organizing: Canadian Experiences.* Toronto: Oxford University Press, 29-61.

Parton, N., D. Thorpe, and C. Wattam. 1997. *Child Protection, Risk and the Moral Order.* London: MacMillan.

Quebec, Minister of Health and Social Services. 1999a. *Act Respecting Health Services and Social Services* (LQ, 1991: Chapter 42, art.80, cited in *Annual Report* CLSC CDN: 8).

——. 1999b. Reference Manual on Youth Protection: Task Force on the Revision of the Youth Protection Act.

Shragge, E. 1999. "Looking Backwards To Go Forward: The Quebec Community Movement 30 Years Later," *Intervention* 110: 53-60.

Shragge, E., and J.M. Fontan. 2000. "Workfare and Community Economic Development in Montreal: Community and Work in the Late Twentieth Century," in P. Hamel, H. Lustiger-Thaler, and M. Mayer, eds., *Urban Movements in a Globalizing World.* London: Routledge, 123-38.

Swift, K. 1995. *Manufacturing Bad Mothers.* Toronto: University of Toronto Press.

Wharf, B., ed. 1993. *Rethinking Child Welfare in Canada.* Toronto: McClelland and Stewart.

White, D. 1991. "Contradictory Participation: Reflections on Community Action in Quebec," in B. Wharf and M. Clague, *Community Organizing: Canadian Experiences.* Toronto: Oxford University Press.

4

Community Organizing in Child Welfare

part one ───────────────────────────────

COMMUNITY ORGANIZING IN CHILD WELFARE: CHANGING
LOCAL ENVIRONMENTS AND DEVELOPING COMMUNITY
CAPACITY

BRAD MCKENZIE

Introduction

Community organization remains somewhat a marginalized program
within urban child welfare agencies, yet it has not disappeared entirely.
For example, Lee (1999 and Chapter 7) documents the persistence of
a community work approach in the Children's Aid Society of Toronto,
and Hudson (1999) relates the evolution of a community organization[1]
approach in Winnipeg Child and Family Services (CFS) since 1985,
with particular attention to its more recent configuration within this
city-wide agency. Hudson's (1999) article documented the early planning process, which precipitated the development of the program during
a period of agency reorganization. He also raised questions about how
the community organization function could be integrated within the
agency's direct service functions and whether this could contribute to
a reformist approach to child welfare services that valued service users
as citizens rather than as clients.

This chapter describes the community organization model that has
emerged in Winnipeg CFS since this planning stage, including a more
detailed discussion of services provided by this program component.
The model reflects an approach to community work that may be

described as locality development (see Chapter 1); however, it does embrace activities related to advocacy and social action.

Most of the information for this case study was collected from written documents and an interview with the manager[2] of the "Community-Based Early Intervention Programs" Unit. Descriptive material was then reviewed by the manager to ensure the accuracy of the following summary.

The Evolution of Community Organizing in Winnipeg Child and Family Services

Winnipeg CFS is a mandated child welfare agency with more than 500 staff serving an urban population in excess of 600,000. While the agency is technically a non-government organization (NGO), the majority of its board members are appointed by government and virtually all funding is provided by government.

The community organization program in Winnipeg CFS was first established in 1985 at a time when six regionalized community-based agencies were created as an alternative to the highly centralized service model established by the Winnipeg Children's Aid Society. At that time "community development" was identified as a method that could build more collaborative working relationships with community, stimulate community involvement and promote the development of community-based prevention and early intervention initiatives. Community organization workers were seen as important in the shift to a more community-oriented model of child welfare practice under regionalization, and the new structure involved a major emphasis on decentralization and the development of elected community boards. Between 1985 and 1991 community workers within each of the six agencies carried out functions that differed markedly from region to region within the city. In some cases these functions were carried out from resource centres that sponsored early intervention outreach programs, became a place for individuals and groups to meet, and provided information and referral services. In other cases community organizing involved efforts to address broader social issues such as housing and child poverty.

Community organization activities contributed to the expansion of prevention and early intervention under regionalization (McKenzie, 1991), but the election of the Conservative government and questions about the continuing efficacy of community outreach in the face of burgeoning child protection caseloads began to affect the integrity of the program by 1990. In 1991, the six regionalized agencies were disbanded, and child welfare services were again centralized under one administrative structure. Between 1991 and 1998, the city was divided into four geographical districts, although area offices and sub-offices within each district maintained some aspects of the community-based service model adopted under regionalization. Community organization positions were retained in the new structure but their numbers dwindled over time, and the importance attached to this work was eroded. There was also a general reduction in the emphasis on community-based services as child welfare services in Winnipeg renewed their historical focus on the investigation and placement functions associated with child protection. This retreat was hastened by media coverage of the death of a baby who had been returned by Winnipeg CFS to her father and his common-law wife (Kuxhaus, 1997).

A new organizational process was launched in 1998, and this led to the adoption of a more specialized service model, including separate, agency-wide service units, each with their own senior manager. This restructuring process placed an increased emphasis on the community organization function in the agency in that a unit known as "Community-Based Early Intervention Programs" was created with its own program manager. Thus, community organizers, previously dispersed within other administrative units, now report to this manager, who is a member of the management team. The unit is composed of 30 staff, or just over 10 per cent of the agency's professional positions. Most of these staff have professional qualifications in social work. While staff are dispersed throughout the city, the unit meets as a group and has an approved mission statement that identifies major goals, objectives, and examples of activities to be carried out in support of its mission statement. The mission statement, which stresses partnerships "to ensure a climate that supports and promotes healthy individuals, families and communities and reduces risks for communities" contains explicit reference to the role of community social work in child welfare within an overall emphasis on prevention and the promotion of community capacity building.

Community Organization Activities

Three somewhat separate functions are carried out by the Community-Based Early Intervention Unit. One involves functions related to volunteer co-ordination. Five staff are engaged in these activities, and there are more than 500 volunteers providing various kinds of services on behalf of the agency. While many volunteers provide support services to individuals or families, others are involved in community service functions such as the community kitchen, and other outreach programs. A second function involves school-linked services, and there are four staff engaged in these activities. Located in selected schools, these staff provide some direct services to children and families, but they also develop and co-ordinate local programs for parents and children. One of the most successful of these projects is the Tri-Agency Program, a co-operative initiative between the school system, the Child Guidance Clinic and the agency. This program responds to the needs of children at risk of violence through work with both children and parents who are engaged as active participants in the process.

All other staff within the unit carry the title "community workers"; however, roles are somewhat dependent on assigned functions, staff skills, and orientation, and neighbourhood needs and priorities. For example, five staff are employed as neighbourhood parent support networkers. These staff and their functions were absorbed by the agency based on the positive outcomes demonstrated by the pilot project on neighbourhood support networks (Fuchs, 1995). The role of these workers has expanded beyond that associated with building support networks for isolated parents, and includes a variety of functions associated with locality development and advocacy. A formal evaluation of this service is being conducted by the agency, and while results are not yet available, there is encouraging evidence of the impact of this program. For example, these workers have not only expanded the mutual aid, helping networks within neighbourhoods, but also assisted these networks in advocacy-oriented activities on issues such as the need for improved housing.

In reviewing the activities of these workers, two important trends were noted. First, it has taken a great deal of time to build trust and establish relationships within neighbourhoods. Second, the model appears to be more successful in communities with some common issues or characteristics that serve as a focal point for networking and community-building. For example, small community-operated resource centres have been established in three neighbourhoods with public housing units, and the agency's community organizing efforts appear to be more successful in these communities than in more transitory or anomic neighbourhoods. Within the three housing developments, the resource centres have become a focal point for parenting programs, network building, and the informal organizing of meetings on advocacy-related issues.

Community organizers are also engaged in two other major functions: the co-ordination of various types of formal support and parenting programs; and more traditional community development work. In the latter case activities are focussed on local community capacity building projects, such as the organization of community kitchens or drop-in centres. However, staff are also engaged in advocacy in response to macro-level issues like poverty and inadequate housing. Three major community resource centres have been established. While a number of the staff work from these resource centres, others have office space in some of the Family Service Units or in other community settings. In addition to agency-based resource centres noted above, staff have been instrumental in developing some smaller independent resource offices managed by a community board or group of volunteers within housing units or local neighbourhoods.

Assessing Effectiveness

Lee (1999) articulates six major objectives in a community approach to practice in child welfare that can contribute to empowered communities. These are citizen participation, organization development, the development of concrete resources for a community, the rediscovery or establishment of a sense of community, social learning, and action on social justice issues. The effectiveness of the community organization program in Winnipeg CFS over the past couple of years is difficult to assess but there is some evidence of beneficial results in relation to a number of these objectives.

The agency has community workers in 12 of the 17 high-need areas of the city, and their impact is clearly identifiable in at least some of these areas. In one case the intervention led to the evolution of a community-based resource centre, now operated by local parents in a low-income housing unit noted for its high rate of social problems and the high number of child protection referrals. The resource centre has been a mobilizing force within the community and issues pertaining to housing and neighbourhood safety have been addressed along with parenting and other concerns related to child welfare. The community-based location of the resource centre and the fact that it is not directly involved in child protection functions makes it a welcome place for local parents. The annual referrals for child abuse and neglect gradually have dropped to almost zero.

Neighbourhood support networkers are active in several communities, and new programs, including partnerships with other agencies and community groups, have helped to change the views of some members of the community about the agency and its general role. While the level of advocacy-related initiatives remains modest, a new advocacy policy is being developed that will sanction a broader range of advocacy efforts on behalf of clients.

Three factors have combined to enhance the role of community organizing in the agency. First, the appointment of a manager for the program has had an influence on internal agency dynamics. As a member of the management group, she is in a position both to advocate for a more community-oriented approach to service development and to provide support to community organization staff in realizing this goal. Second, the philosophy of a community-based early intervention program is consistent with that of the present provincial government, and this is reflected in some related government-sponsored initiatives. For example, funding has been provided for the development of community-based family resource centres. Third, the program has received positive feedback on a number of its initiatives, including the agency's ability to engage with the community in a role other than that associated with the social-control functions in child welfare.

The Future of Community Organization in Winnipeg's Child Welfare System

Two major limitations in the agency's service model may have an impact on the future of the program within the agency. One concerns the limited involvement of the local community in the governance structure of the agency. The agency's centralized board is dominated by government appointees although there is one representative from each of the four geographically defined Area Councils that function as advisory bodies to the agency. However, given the centralized organizational structure of the agency these Area Councils have very little influence on agency policy or service development. While specific initiatives, like resource centres, may establish community advisory committees, these bodies provide advice and direction only in relation to these particular initiatives. Because of the limited mandate of these committees and the Area Advisory Councils, there is little formal linkage to the community on matters of general agency policy or service direction. Thus, the general community does not function as a general advocate for a more community-oriented model of service as it did under regionalization between 1985 and 1990.

A second, and somewhat related problem, pertains to the interface between the activities of community organizers and the work of other staff who are more directly involved in child protection functions. The experience here is mixed. There are examples of family service workers who consult with neighbourhood parent support workers on child protection issues, and some community workers have established close working relationships with protection staff serving particular areas of the city. But in many areas intake is assigned on a rotational rather than geographic basis and it is practically impossible to co-ordinate neighbourhood-based services under these circumstances. In addition, there appears to be little evidence that most service units place a high priority on developing close working relationships with community organization staff or in developing a more community-based approach to service delivery.

At the time of this writing there was considerable uncertainty about the future child welfare service delivery system in the city of Winnipeg. In one of the most significant social policy initiatives in the province over the past several decades, the NDP government, elected in 1999, has signed separate Memorandums of Understanding with the Manitoba Métis Federation and the two umbrella First Nations governance structures in the province. These agreements include a government commitment to transfer service responsibility for off-reserve Aboriginal child welfare services to these Aboriginal authorities. Within the City of Winnipeg, between 60 and 70 per cent of the children in care are Aboriginal and this restructuring process will have major implications for the configuration of child and family services in the city. While a general policy commitment has been made, the parties are currently engaged in a planning process and working groups are examining a number of operational issues, including funding and service delivery models. One impediment is that the current socioeconomic climate is resistant to new investment in social programs, and as expected, resource needs for a major policy shift of this nature are proving to be a major stumbling block.

It is anticipated that implementation of the policy change will occur gradually and will involve a reduced role for Winnipeg Child and Family Services. It is also likely that the new service delivery model adopted by Aboriginal authorities will place more emphasis on community-based prevention and early intervention services, a direction that is consistent with the philosophy of the current provincial government and the agency's Community-Based Early Intervention Unit. While these developments may serve to enhance the profile of community organizing within the city's child welfare system, there are obvious risks for Winnipeg CFS. First, there is the risk that an accelerated planning process coupled with inadequate resources for policy implementation will lead to an immediate reduction in resources for Winnipeg Child and Family Services as funds are diverted to the new Aboriginal-controlled system. Such reductions may affect the agency's continuing ability to fund its community organization program. A second, and somewhat related issue, is the potential backlash that can emerge from some segments of the community in response to a paradigm shift that places more emphasis on family support and less emphasis on the investigative function in child welfare. When these transitions are coupled with scarce resources, questions of risk and the well-being of children are frequently raised, and it is not uncommon for these concerns to lead eventually to a renewed emphasis on risk assessment and "case management."

Implications for Best Practices

This case study also examined implications for best practice in the programs and services currently being delivered by the agency. The notion of "best practice" in community organizing is often associated with qualities and processes that contribute to effectiveness in community work interventions. These are essential but insufficient in establishing a community work presence within child welfare. Some of the factors emerging from this case study include the need for clarity in the role and functions to be performed and the importance of training and skills in community organizing. An ability to define one's role relative to the agency and the community is assisted by an appropriate mandate for the program. A mission statement and program goals can help to legitimize this role but the commitment of the organization must be expressed by ongoing support that gives meaning to general principles and goal statements. In the case of Winnipeg CFS this has been reinforced through the role of a program manager who is a member of the management team.

While professional skills and training in community work are important it was observed that a more fundamental ingredient was a strong commitment to social change, and the importance of both individual and collective responses to social injustice. Social work graduates often did not possess this combination of both reasoned anger about the system and the skills to work collaboratively with clients and communities in promoting social change. This may reflect a shortcoming in the generalist orientation of most undergraduate social work programs or the ideological impact of models of practice that appear preoccupied with specialized techniques such as risk assessment and solution-focussed counselling.

There are other challenges to incorporating a community organization function within child welfare. One is the expectation that effective community organizing can be accomplished in a short period of time. If one is working within communities where community support networks have broken down and there are a number of social problems, it takes a great deal of time to establish trust and build relationships. It takes an even longer time to implement an agenda for change. This process of social learning and action is enhanced by staff continuity and an ability to develop relationships based on mutual respect. Results are also somewhat dependent on the characteristics of communities in that those experiencing anomie and more pervasive feelings of powerlessness are much more difficult to organize. On the other hand, the presence of even a limited number of committed local leaders makes a critical difference. Another important factor is whether other service professionals working in the area are willing to collaborate in developing a community-oriented approach to empowerment.

Although it is difficult to establish the relative influence of each factor in promoting the success of community work in child welfare, this case study demonstrates the importance of each of the following: organizational commitment and support, the development of program goals and technology, staff commitment and skills, the presence of other allied professionals committed to collaborative work, and community or neighbourhood characteristics.

In reflecting on the experience of Winnipeg CFS, it is apparent that the profile of community work has been enhanced over the past two years, but that it is not well integrated within agency operations or service delivery teams. To a significant extent, the agency's current service delivery model, which has discarded community-based service delivery teams in favour of specialized city-wide units, is inconsistent with a more integrated community-oriented approach. While the philosophy and goals of the community work unit is sanctioned within the agency, this remains as the mission of the unit rather than the agency. The adoption of a more community-building philosophy for the agency, and its integration into the operations of other services yet remains an elusive goal. While major transformation may be unlikely, there are two potential factors that could encourage further movement in this direction. One is the growing recognition of the contributions being made by the community organization unit, and a second is the current political climate within both government and Aboriginal agencies, which appears to support a more community-oriented approach to the provision of child and family services.

notes

1. The term "community organizing" is used here for reasons outlined in Chapter 1, although the terms "community work" and "community development" are often used within the agency and convey the same meaning.

2. The author wishes to acknowledge Sue Hudson, the Program Manager for the Community-Based Intervention Program Unit, for the information provided on activities and impact of the unit. The views expressed about the program and its future are those of the author.

references

Fuchs, D. 1995. "Preserving and Strengthening Families and Protecting Children: Social Network Intervention, A Balanced Approach to the Prevention of Child Maltreatment," in J. Hudson and B. Galaway, eds., *Child Welfare in Canada: Research and Policy Implications*. Toronto: Thompson Educational Publishing, 113-39.

Hudson, P. 1999. "Community Development and Child Protection: A Case for Integration." *Community Development Journal* 34,4: 346-55.

Kuxhaus, D. 1997. "CFS failed Sophia: Judge," *Winnipeg Free Press* (25 Jan.): A1.

Lee, B. 1999. "A Community Approach to Urban Child Welfare in Canada," in L. Dominelli, ed., *Community Approaches to Child Welfare: International Perspectives*. Aldershot, Hampshire: Ashgate, 64-87.

McKenzie, B. 1991. "Decentralization in Winnipeg: Assessing the Effects of Community-Based Child Welfare Services," *Canadian Review of Social Policy* 27: 57-66.

part two ──

CHILD PROTECTION THROUGH STRENGTHENING COMMUNITIES: THE TORONTO CHILDREN'S AID SOCIETY

BILL LEE & SHARRON RICHARDS

Purpose

The Community Development[1] and Prevention Program of the Children's Aid Society of Toronto (CAST) has been in existence for over 30 years. For a community work program anywhere, let alone one that "resides" in a child welfare setting, this is a significant accomplishment, as community-oriented programs are not the norm in child welfare (Lee, 1999b). The phenomenon of this longevity has stimulated a number of discussions, most of them informal among some academics, present and past workers, as well as community activists who have come in contact with the program.[2]

The purpose here is to present the thinking of the authors, both of whom have been at the centre of the majority of such discussions. Prior to joining the School of Social Work at McMaster University, Lee worked with the program in the early 1970s and has over the last 20 years maintained a relationship through support and education. Richards worked with the program from 1974 until 1981. Currently she manages the program. What the authors offer here is not a formal study of the workings of the program but our analysis of our experiences of the program aided by what we have heard over the years from various colleagues and reports from the CAST program itself. While there are a number of unique features in the CAST history and development, we have identified five that seem to us to be significant. One of the key factors is the manner in which the program has been able to institutionalize itself and become increasingly understood and accepted within the agency. A second factor is the particular receptivity and commitment of the CAST to allocating resources to engage in primary prevention activities. The third factor is the prevention orientation of the provincial child welfare legislation under which the program was initially conceived and has co-operated. The fourth factor is the breadth of its approach to community work. Using Rothman and Tropman's framework (1987) we can see that the program has utilized a wide array of approaches in its work. This flexibility, we believe, has allowed it to adapt and be relevant to changing social, economic, and political conditions. Finally, as well as institutionalizing itself within the CAST, it has also managed to become an important player in the community at large. The work that has been accomplished with communities has provided the program with a level of community support that has been crucial to its development and survival.

One of the prevailing trends in social welfare today is the interest in seeing community take a more central focus in the strategies to combat social problems. While McKnight (1995) is probably the best-known of the writers who espouse the importance of community, there are many others in Canada (e.g., Carniol, 1999; Lee, 1999a; Wharf, 1997) and abroad (Ife, 1998) who argue that attention to larger social issues should occupy a central place in dealing with problems faced by individuals and families. More specifically, there is a growing, though perhaps unclear, understanding that the well-being of children depends not only on the physical and mental well-being of their caregivers but also on the strength of the social, economic, and political networks in which they live (National Council of Welfare, 1998). Poverty, unemployment, inadequate housing, lack of community cohesion, discrimination, racism, and sexism are seen to contribute to the difficulties faced by the families involved with child protection services. At the same time, child welfare in Canada, as in other jurisdictions, is specified essentially in terms of work with families and children whose troubles are defined as existing primarily in the realm of the personal (Lee, 1999b; Macintyre, 1993). Thus, the recognition of the importance of structural factors notwithstanding, the application of a community organization approach by the CAST remains unusual, even marginal. While it does not represent the only child welfare program that exists and has existed in Ontario—there are and have been small community work efforts in Ontario since the 1970s[3]— it is fair to say that the CAST program represents the only consistent long-term community development approach in Ontario.

Program Background

The Children's Aid Society of Toronto (CAST) is the largest, board-operated[4] child welfare agency in North America. In 1999 it served 9,015 families and 23,978 children and youth, of whom 20,582 received services while living at home, and 3,396 were provided with foster or residential care. Emergency After Hours Service was received by 13,072 children and families, resulting in 460 emergency admissions to care. CAST has an approximate complement of 674 staff positions, 370 foster families and 580 volunteers. The 1998-99 budget was $95.5 million, which is funded fully by the provincial government (CAST, 1999). The profile of the families served reveals the following:

- 56 per cent are single parents compared to 14.5 per cent of all Canadian families and 13 per cent of Ontario families;

- Approximately 73 per cent live at or below the poverty line;

- 53 per cent receive some form of social assistance;

- 23 per cent live in social housing, and an estimated 7 per cent live in shelters, temporary accommodation, or are homeless;

- 47 per cent of families and 37 per cent of children/youth in care self-identify as a member of a minority culture or race;

- 69 per cent of parents are assessed as having a mental health problem;

- 40 per cent abuse drugs and/or alcohol;

- 60 per cent of parents are victims of abuse and maltreatment;

- 20 per cent of families experience domestic violence, which frequently is witnessed by the children;

- the number of impoverished in the City of Toronto is double that for the rest of Ontario, and about as many poor children live in Toronto as in all Atlantic Canada (CAST, 1999).

The CAST has a long tradition of assuming stances relative to issues of social justice, particularly when they are believed to be important to the lives of children and families. This created an agency culture that was amenable to the introduction of community work as part of the spectrum of child welfare services provided by CAST. While other child welfare organizations certainly involved themselves in collaboration with other service agencies (Lee,1999b), the CAST program, from its inception, took a more grassroots approach to community work, engaging residents in disadvantaged communities and neighbourhoods.

In the late 1960s, CAST acknowledged that the impact of social, economic, and political conditions on the incidence of child abuse, neglect, and family breakdown could not be fully addressed at the individual and family level. Provincial child welfare legislation also reflected this belief as set out in the Child and Family Services Act by legislating the child welfare mandate to include not only the protection of children but also *"the prevention of circumstances requiring the protection of children"* (Section 15 [3] C; emphasis added). One of the ways in which the CAST began to implement the prevention mandate was to establish an agency-wide community work program. As indicated in Chapter 1, it began with the designation of two protection staff having time allotted to engage in community work in two social housing communities. Based on the success of that experience, additional workers were hired as "community protection workers," meaning they carried a three-fifths caseload comprised of protection caseload and two-fifths of community work activities. In the 1970s and early 1980s there were 10 program staff with two workers assigned to each of CAST's five geographic branches. The community work staff were supervised in the branch by supervisors who were neither trained nor experienced in the community approach to social work. To respond to the need for the program staff to access consultation and support from those experienced in and knowledgeable about community work, the agency established the Cross Branch Community Work Group. It met every second week and was comprised of the eight community workers and, on occasion, their supervisors. Currently there are six full-time Community Development and Prevention Program staff, and in 1994 the Program was centralized under one supervisor, whose background includes community development work.

While the Program has had a long history of supporting community capacity-building across the City of Toronto, that history includes its share of challenges. Throughout the late 1970s and early 1980s, the program was implemented by two community workers assigned to each of the Society's five geographic branches. The current complement is one worker per branch, one position assigned agency-wide, and one centralized supervisory position. The positions of Prevention Team supervisor and Society Child Welfare Advocate are combined in one worker, funded by the Children's Aid Foundation. Over the years, in response to funding realities, Program staff has been reduced by almost 50 per cent, while Toronto's population has grown both in actual numbers and in the diversity of its citizenship.

Today, the Community Development and Prevention Program reflects the Society's commitment, as stated in its mission and values (CAST, 1997) to engage in "developing, in partnership with others, prevention programmes, which encourage healthy and positive relationships among children and their families within their communities" while providing "leadership and advocacy in developing solutions to child welfare issues" (ibid.). The Program also has been instrumental in allowing the Society to make operational Board policies related to prevention and advocacy.

Within the context of community development practice in a child welfare setting, Program staff have defined child maltreatment intervention as:

> Promotion of activities that reduce the incidence of child maltreatment and neglect by enabling communities to support children, youth and families:
>
> (a) At the local level, by minimizing risk factors, promoting competencies, maximizing the development of children and youth and enhancing the quality of life;
>
> (b) At the societal level, by promoting policy/program change to create the social, economic and legal equality that promotes healthy families and communities. (Ibid.)

Program Activities

The CAST's Community Work Program has always engaged in all three areas of community development activities: locality development, social planning, and social action (Rothman and Tropman, 1987). The balance of activities within each area varies among Program staff according to their individual skill and interest; the uniqueness of the community with whom they are engaged; and the prevailing social, economic, and political environment. In the 1960s and 1970s, the focus of involvement was predominantly on facilitating and supporting community capacity to develop community-based programs, resources, and organizations designed to support children, youth, and families. These resources were and continue to be resident-identified, directed, organized, and managed. Funding shifts and cutbacks in the 1980s saw a program shift to engage in more social action or "issue organizing" both in local communities and more broadly—municipally, provincially, and federally. A report from that period stated: "Based on our collective experience over the past couple of years, the Cross Branch Community Work Group is proposing that future community work activity be structured to allow a co-ordinated approach to common issues at both the local and Metro levels" (Cross Branch Community Work Group, 1980). This approach would focus on those problems that are threatening to cripple the very ability of families to survive—housing, daycare, illiteracy, levels of social assistance. Currently, in response to the significant reduction in funding at all government levels, there is an even greater imbalance in the activity level of the Program, but most specifically between locality development and social justice activities.

LOCALITY DEVELOPMENT

The local neighbourhoods and communities with whom CAST community work staff are engaged can be described as at risk, disadvantaged, and vulnerable. They are communities with common geography, interest, culture, ethnicity, race, or newness to the City of Toronto. Most are social housing communities, with a high proportion of single parents and low income families, many of whom are immigrants or refugees. Often, the communities have been identified for community development intervention because of the disproportionate number of families receiving child welfare services. Communities of interest may include young mothers, youth, social assistance recipients, public housing tenants, and ethnocultural groups. Toronto is reported to be one of the most culturally and ethnically diverse cities in the world and that diversity is reflected in the new and emerging communities whom Program staff are increasingly called upon to support.

The results of locality development work on the part of Program staff are visible through the creation of family resource centres, early childhood development programs, youth shelters, after-school programs, legal aid services, parent support programs, social recreation programs, substance abuse prevention programs for children and youth, community economic development services, and programs designed to support immigrant and refugee families.

Examples include the Brahms Bike Club in the former City of North York. The Bike Club is a community economic development project operated by community residents with support from the CAST branch community worker, the police department, and staff from Parks and Recreation and the Public Housing Authority. Local children and youth learn about how to repair bikes, bicycle safety, and how to work and play together. The Brahms Bike Club has recently been chosen as a recipient of one of the City of Toronto's Neighbourhood Awards. The Children's Aid Foundation is one of the funders for this project. A second example is the Somali Immigrant Women's Organization, which has called upon the CAST to provide community work support to help them develop a parent drop-in program in the former City of Etobicoke where large numbers of Somali families reside. The community worker is assisting the group to access funding, as well as linking the volunteers running the program to existing parent drop-in programs from whom they can learn and get support. A third example is Scarborough's Success By Six Program, a collaboration among a variety of community-based organizations serving young children and their families. It is funded by the United Way. The CAST program component is the provision of parenting programs for parents involved with the agency who have been ordered by Child Welfare Court to attend a parenting education course.

SOCIAL PLANNING

An example of a social planning activity is the Lakeshore Community Audit, an initiative of community residents, local agencies, the City of Toronto, the Community and Social Planning Council, and funded by the Ontario Trillium Foundation. The audit was conducted throughout the Lakeshore community, which is located in the southwest area of the new Toronto, in the former city of Etobicoke. "The goal of the audit was to: improve the quality of life through participatory research; build leadership, launch community initiatives" (Lakeshore Area Multi Service Project, 1999). Currently, there are approximately 176 families receiving child protection services from CAST in this geographic community of 25,969 households.

The CAST's community worker assigned to the Society's Etobicoke branch played an active role on the Steering Committee of the Lakeshore Audit Project (LCAP). In that role he supported the work of the Committee, challenged the researchers to be sensitive to the needs of community residents from diverse backgrounds and helped organize events related to the release of the audit's Report Card, including a press conference and two community forums. He continues to be involved with the initiative, which is now focussed on local actions to improve the quality of life in the Lakeshore Community. One of these is a housing support program whose goal is to match families experiencing a housing problem with affordable and appropriate housing.

SOCIAL ACTION

Child welfare in Ontario had its beginning in the 1800s when a young *Toronto Telegram* reporter named J.J. Kelso became a vocal advocate on behalf of the abused and neglected children found on Toronto's streets. The CAST has a long and distinguished history of advocating on behalf of children, youth, and families. The Community Program, therefore, plays a significant role in promoting the "best interests" of children through the involvement of staff in a variety of social action/social justice activities.

Individual staff members have, over the years, developed expertise in special areas of focus such as family income and child poverty, housing, child care, immigration and refugee issues, and access and equity to services. Much of the social action work is carried out as members of social justice coalitions such as: the Child Poverty Action Group; Metro Campaign 2000; Public Housing Fight Back Group; Home Front Coalition; Metro Coalition for Better Child Care; Metro Association of Family Resources Centres; Metro Network For Social Justice; the Immigration and Refugee Advisory Committee; Children's Action Committee of the City of Toronto; the Access and Equity Task Force of the City of Toronto.

Influencing public policy and the allocation of public resources is frequently the focus of this activity. Program staff are called upon to support the work of a coalition through such activities as administrative support; human resource development; group facilitation; planning; fundraising; co-ordinating the preparation of position papers; "report card" writing; co-ordinating letter-writing campaigns; organizing public awareness and social justice events; public speaking; organizing and presenting at community information forums; preparation of press releases; organizing and participating in press conferences; writing letters on behalf of CAST regarding specific social justice issues; and assisting with the development of CAST board policies related to specific social issues: housing, child care, workfare, and education.

Over the years, the social action work performed by CAST's community work staff in coalitions has been able to influence public policy and political decisions that impact on the children, youth, and families served by child welfare. Some examples are: the introduction of rent controls in the 1980s; the introduction of human rights legislation prohibiting discrimination by landlords against families with children; the increase in funding for the federal Child Tax Benefit; provincial funding for child care direct grants; preventing the introduction of recreation user fees for children and youth in the recently amalgamated City of Toronto; and a recent decision by the Ontario Municipal Board to uphold a city "second suites" zoning bylaw allowing for apartments in single-family dwellings.

The involvement of CAST's community work staff in all three models of community work makes it relatively unique in Toronto. While there are numerous agencies practicing community development, they tend to focus more on one model than on all three. It has been the experience of Program staff that engaging in all three models allows residents to understand local issues within the context of city-wide, provincial, and national issues. It creates a link between the impact of broader public policy on individual children, youth, and families and the communities in which they live. It also increases opportunities for residents from different communities across Toronto to come together to address common problems and to share and learn from each other's achievements and successes.

The community work program is committed to the focus on community issues as a means of developing strengthened environments for children and families and has striven to be innovative as well as productive in addressing this goal. Its experience can offer board members and administrators of direct service agencies some opportunities to think about the potential of examining prevention from a wider viewpoint than simply that of early intervention or more decentralized programming. To do this, however, we need to suggest some of the challenges as well as the payoffs.

Benefits

COMMUNITY

Significant benefits have resulted from the community development approach within Children's Aid Society of Toronto. Utilizing the work of one of the authors of this paper (Lee, 1999a; 1999b) we can suggest five important areas where community life has been positive.

CITIZEN PARTICIPATION: This refers to an increase in the quantity and quality of the members' involvement in community life. Participation can be understood as an antidote to social alienation (Lee, 1999a) and a key aspect of citizenship (Lee et al., 2000). Local residents become actively involved in community life through their participation in community needs assessments, community capacity mapping, program planning, fundraising, organizing community events, and organizational development. For many of the community residents, who have experienced a sense of isolation and feelings of being disenfranchised, this may be the first time that they have become involved in any kind of civic participation. They not only contribute to the life of the community, but benefit as individuals as well. They can begin to experience an increased sense of involvement, increased self-confidence, increased feelings of competence, an awareness of belonging and connection to their neighbours, as well as improved self-esteem. They begin to build, both within and outside the immediate community, networks and support systems that will benefit their children and themselves. The skills and capacities individuals develop through their participation in the community building process are seen as transferable to improved personal and parenting relationships. When parents begin to participate in the civic life of the community, they are more likely to encourage their children to become involved in community activities as well. An example of individual empowerment through civic participation is Toronto resident Wanda MacNevin, who has become a community activist and professional health promoter in the Jane-Finch community where she has resided for the last 30 years.[5]

ORGANIZATIONAL DEVELOPMENT: This refers to creating new or strengthening existing organizations or groups within the community, that provide services or allow people to come together to identify and discuss issues. The aim here is not service agencies but local group formation wherein local civic participation may be experienced. These community organizations provide places for members to meet and the opportunities to learn and volunteer their time, to give as well as to receive from their neighbours.

One of the objectives of community development is to build on the capacities and strengths of local residents to create programs, resources, and organizations that families and residents can access for support and assistance. The community development worker's role is to facilitate a process through which community residents learn to develop, plan, implement, and manage the programs and organizations they create. These community infrastructures may include tenant associations, community resident councils, program management committees, and boards of directors. The ultimate goal of the community development worker is to be able to leave the community knowing the community residents have developed the experience and skills to sustain the community infrastructures they have helped build.

The Jane-Finch Community and Family Centre is an example. It began in the 1970s with a group of residents coming together, with support from one of CAST's North York branch community workers, to address common issues of concern in their community. It went on to become an incorporated, non-profit community organization, which today offers a variety of services, programs, and resources to residents in the Jane-Finch community. The CAST community worker played an instrumental role in helping community members incorporate, access funding, hire and manage staff, develop a board of directors, and plan and implement programs and services.

COMMUNITY SENSE: This means an improvement in the ability of community members, as a collective, to deal with issues facing them. Too often the neighbourhoods and communities in which CAST's community workers are active are viewed negatively. It is not uncommon to describe one community by comparing it to another community with a negative image or reputation for experiencing a number of social problems. In Toronto, an example would be to refer to a community as a "Regent Park" or a "Jane-Finch," two high-density, low-income communities, perceived by the general public and the media to be "problem" communities. The former is Canada's oldest social housing community and the latter is a community of mixed housing. While the "outside world" sometimes sees these communities in a negative light, community residents take pride in the significant amount of community building that has taken place over the years. That coming together of people to take control in order to improve the quality of community life is a powerful experience that assists people to feel a sense of community belonging and pride. Where we live is often associated with how we're respected and valued, making a sense of community pride important to our general sense of well-being. In 1998, Regent Park residents celebrated the fiftieth anniversary of community accomplishments and civic participation. The celebration was planned and organized by community residents and included activities for all ages and cultures. The Children's Aid Foundation provided some financial support to this celebration.

SOCIAL LEARNING: A community development process allows for residents to increase their learning at the individual, community, and broader public policy level. Individuals are called upon to use a range of often untapped capacities and skills (McKnight, 1995). It can involve developing the capacity to engage in door-knocking; developing and conducting community surveys; preparing and delivering community information workshops; organizing community events; writing fundraising proposals; planning and implementing programs for community children, youth, parents, and seniors; and organizing advocacy campaigns. At the individual skill level, residents who are involved in community capacity-building develop and/or enhance their skills in interpersonal communication, presentation, organization, mediation, and conflict resolution.

Such is the case with public housing tenants who have come together in the Public Housing Fight Back Group to prevent the sale by the provincial government of public housing units in Toronto to the private sector. The CAST community worker with a lead responsibility for housing has assisted the Group to reach out to public housing tenants, plan public education activities, prepare for and present their position to the Board of Directors of the Toronto Housing Authority, and link with other housing advocacy groups addressing the needs of public housing tenants. Another example is the recently formed Parents Action Network, comprised of parents, predominantly women, interested in giving a voice and a face to the struggles and challenges faced by many sole-support, low-income parents. The participants learned how to plan and organize a picnic at the provincial legislature to call attention to the negative impact of provincial policies and legislation on children, youth, and families. It is anticipated that they will also be involved in learning how to make public presentations, deal with the media, and become public spokespersons.

Communities learn that when residents speak as a collective voice there is more likelihood of being heard. They experience that by coming together to address community-wide issues they can make a difference. They also learn that as a community they share responsibility for each other's welfare and well-being. For example, in child welfare, child abuse is understood as a community responsibility. Community development is a concrete way in which a child welfare agency can partner with the community to support and assist members to take on responsibility for preventing and dealing with child abuse. The resources and programs created or accessed through developmental process contribute to reduced family stress, enhanced parenting capacity, increased family support networks, and increased opportunities for healthy child development. Communities not only increase their capacity to support families through local, community-based programs and resources, they also become skilled at addressing the public policy legislation and funding that is not in the best interests of children.

RESOURCES: This refers to acquiring or improving useful facilities and/or services for the community. Resources or improved access are seen to spring from local activity. As well, the acquisition of local resources allows for the potential for increased local management of problems and reflects back to members their ability to influence their environment. The number of identifiable, concrete resources, programs, and community-based organizations that have been created over the past 30 years across Toronto as a result of the involvement of CAST community staff are numerous. They include: the Jane-Finch Family and Child Centre; Mornelle Family Resource Centre; Swansea Mews Youth Counselling Program; the Brahms Bicycle Club; the Somali Women's and Children's Network Project; Scarborough's Success By Six Project; the York Youth Shelter, Welcome Baby Support Program; Babies Best Start; East End Young Moms Project; Students Tutoring At Rockcliffe (STAR); Metro Campaign 2000; Social Housing Fight Back Group; Collaboration in Community Development; Community Economic Development Learning Network; and the Ontario Coalition for Mandatory Parenting.

Over the course of its history, CAST's Community Work Program has been instrumental in helping Toronto's diverse communities raise millions of dollars for community-based programs and resources. In 1999 Program staff assisted communities to access over $3 billion.

In concluding this section it would be useful to let some individuals say how the program assisted them.

> The community development approach helped us create new community leadership and helped to develop new leaders in the community. The CAS Community Worker provided an overview on issues, logistical and technical support and political analysis as well as support for ourselves. (Bill Worrell, Co-ordinator, Equally Healthy Kids, LAMP Health and Community Service Centre)

> It's very important to us that the CAST is working in a way to develop community so our world will have fewer children at risk. I'm also heartened that CAST workers are using their expertise and information from a variety of sources to help the people who feel marginalized feel more connected

to their community. (Beverley Halls, Parent Action Network participant)

AGENCY

The CAST has also benefited significantly from having the Program as part of its service delivery system. The involvement of Program staff is perceived by community residents as non-threatening, positive, and supportive. This is in contrast to the agency's protective services, which are not always viewed as positively. While not an objective of the program, the activities and benefits experienced by communities as a result of community worker involvement are significant. This is especially the case with many of Toronto's newer, ethno-specific communities, for whom involvement with a child welfare system is unknown and unfamiliar within their cultural context, while community building involvement is a known and familiar experience. Community residents in both established and in new communities may call upon CAST's community work staff to broker or mediate contentious cases when they develop within the other service areas of the agency. Elected politicians who become familiar with Program staff may also look to them, either directly or through their constituency office staff, for information related to a specific case community or to broker a situation in which the politician's office has become involved.

Similarly, throughout the agency staff often call upon the community workers to help them identify and access community-based services and resources for their clients. Often the community worker has knowledge of community-based resources not found in the City's formal information resource systems. As well, the community workers, because of their extensive community contacts, are called upon to assist the agency in recruiting potential board, committee, and focus group members from Toronto's diverse communities.

The development of community resources to support the children, youth, and families involved with CAST's protection and children-in-care services is also an offshoot of the community worker's community contacts. Over the years, indigenous community homes and homemakers have become available to support families where protection concerns are minimal. Community homes are neighbours or families in the community with whom the community worker has established a relationship and who are prepared to provide out-of-home care to children/youth from the same community for short periods of time. The agency brokers the agreement between the parent and the community home parent for the provision of temporary care of the children. The parent pays the community home for the care of the children/youth, with the possibility of the agency subsidizing the arrangement. The same arrangement works for the placement of a community resident as a homemaker in a family for a short, specified period of time. Currently, there is seldom a call for these kind of resources, given the complexity of the family problems requiring CAST intervention.

Challenges

A question raised by the success of the CAST program is: Why is the community approach not found in more jurisdictions? After all, the notion of community is increasingly promoted as an important element in dealing with social problems. John McKnight's (1995) notion of asset-based community strategies in social policy is seen as one of the really important developments in dealing with social problems (McGrath et al., 1999). Like other neo-conservative governments, the present one in Ontario is committed to the belief that individuals and communities can resolve the social problems that affect them. If "community is the answer" or one of the answers, why is it that we do not see more community work programs in child welfare? There are a number of ways to look at this question.

LACK OF COMMUNITY WORK EDUCATION IN SOCIAL WORK

Pointing up Wharf's (1993) assertion that community work occupies a peripheral place in social work, Lee et al. (1997) found that community work in Canadian schools of social work was treated as a marginal subject and given scant attention in comparison with traditional "clinical" approaches. Thus, we can expect that the great majority of social workers emerge from school with a relatively low awareness of the potential of community work. Social work has long been recognized as a conservative profession (Carniol, 1999; Wharf, 1993). Clearly it is important for the field, in dialogue with schools of social work, to identify prevention as an important general focus for education and, specifically, to treat community work as a legitimate strategy.

LACK OF COMMITMENT TO PREVENTION

Prevention is one of those terms that practitioners may speak about with greater ease than that with which they understand it. Community workers in child welfare have been asked typically to engage in program activities—like self-help groups or children's recreation programs. Not that these are not useful activities, but they tend to make a better fit with traditional service provision than with the community work objectives mentioned above. Clearly this is an issue related to the lack of community work attention within social work education. At the same time it should be remembered that even when community work was much more popular and social work education was making a greater attempt to address it, very few community development programs were mounted in child welfare. One wonders to what extent schools of social work would be supported by community agencies (who provide practicum opportunities as well as centres of employment) if community work were provided with a higher profile.

LACK OF CLARITY ABOUT WHAT PREVENTION MEANS

One of the reasons that agencies may not be supportive of community development as prevention might be that the notion of prevention itself is not clear. Does it refer simply to the notion of keeping children out of care? In these terms there are a number of instrumental and affective interventions—the provisions of homemakers in times of crisis and innovative approaches to involving parents in intervention (Jackson and Nixon, 1999)—that might be considered. Or, work on influencing policy at senior levels of staff also can legitimately be considered prevention. The spectrum is a wide one and coupled with the limited understanding of community development and its potential for improving the concrete reality of community life, it may be overlooked by agencies. Added to this, of course, is the fact that any type of prevention method is given a low level of priority by governments—certainly by the present Ontario government—so prevention of any stripe is rarely provided with adequate levels of funding. Thus, it is difficult for hard-pressed agencies who have not had the opportunity to think about the prevention spectrum, and the place of community development within it, to see its potential. Again, this is where schools of social work have a responsibility to address seriously issues of prevention and the role of community work within it.

COMMUNITY WORK AS CONFLICT

Another issue is that community work emerged from its last "heyday" with an image that implied a conflict-oriented methodology. The histories of such practitioners as Saul Alinsky and some projects like the federally funded Company of Young Canadians in the 1960s and 1970s, for example, suggested that community work led to conflict. In fact, there is truth here. Because community work strives to assist groups of citizens advocating for themselves, conflict may sometimes, though not always, be involved. In some situations, it may be necessary (Lee, 1999a). Part of the problem is that little attention is given either to the "uneven" conditions dealt with by marginalized groups or to the institutional coercion (the Ontario government's workfare policy, for example) that requires dramatic action. A second issue is that, in the popular imagination, conflict is often conflated with physical violence. Thus, agency administrators may wish to avoid having to field criticism. Indeed there is a great deal of criticism directed towards child-welfare agencies—from left and right. They may not want to risk having a program that may seem to deliberately "stir the pot." The CAST has shown that it can deal with such a dynamic, but it has taken time for this to become part of its corporate culture. As well, it has involved the determination of the community practitioners who have worked hard to inculcate the values of community work in their settings.

CONSERVATIVE SOCIAL/POLITICAL MILIEU

While politicians and academics may espouse the notion of the importance of community, many of them come at it from a fairly simplistic conservative mentality. Thus, there is a tendency to see—as McKnight (1995) apparently does (see also, McGrath et al., 1999)—voluntary community activity as a necessary antidote to state-supported social services that have undercut people's willingness to act collectively to solve problems. Given the situations that already press against community life— the undercutting of the material base of the community, role changes for women, and increasing diversity to name a few—this is both unrealistic and regressive. Thus, the kind of creative community development approaches that we see in this program and that require a certain level of funding are rarely seriously examined for child welfare. Community work must be seen not only as useful but also in our contemporary context as requiring state funding. Clearly with the present ideologically oriented Ontario government this will be problematic. Ironically, it is the positive relationships that have been built up by CAST's community work staff with the broader community that have often been of assistance in maintaining the Program's existence. It has looked to the community as well as to the agency for its sense of legitimacy.

FUNDING

The question of funding uncertainty raises the issue of the tension between the notion of community organization as an endeavour oriented to structural change and its sponsorship through a quasi-state agency like CAST. Is it possible for Program staff to tackle social and political conditions that threaten the welfare of children and families when the agency is both funded and mandated by government? Clearly, in Western liberal democracies, the governing class is deeply connected to the economic élites and their interests. The fiscal and social policies of the current Ontario government are antithetical to the basic principles of community work, particularly those focussed on social justice issues (Ralph, 1998). The CAST Community Work Program is, however, no stranger to this tension. From its inception it has faced various challenges, especially related to efforts to involve citizens in public policy discussions. In the late 1970s, there was a significant outcry from a municipal politician and one Toronto newspaper regarding the involvement of a CAST community worker's efforts to involve tenants in supporting provincial human rights legislation that would prohibit discrimination by landlords against families with children seeking rental accommodation. Questions were raised as to why, working for a provincially funded body, CAST staff were engaged in what was perceived to be advocacy against the government. CAST's Board and Executive Director stayed the course and supported a child welfare organization's responsibility to advocate on behalf of the children, youth, and families it served.

There have been two responses to this dilemma. First, the workers and managers have worked hard to institutionalize the Program within the agency. This has involved extensive education within the agency as to how prevention fits within the organization's mandate. It has more recently involved the consolidation of the program under one supervisor. Second, the agency has sought to obtain funding outside of government.

AGENCY-SPECIFIC CHALLENGES

In the early years of the Program, when its goals and objectives were not well defined, the community workers often found themselves in conflict with their managers as to who determined the focus of their work. To be effective community workers, the issues to be addressed and actions to be taken must be identified and directed by the community. But if the employing agency believes it directs program activities, the community workers can find themselves caught between the two interests. The challenge, then, is for organizations to be clear about how community work is to be practised prior to bringing community work staff into its service delivery system.

Prior planning should also include careful consideration of workload expectations for community workers. For many years, Program staff had a split workload of both protection cases and community work activities. The combination proved to be unmanageable within a child welfare setting given the crisis potential of the casework function and the priority that must be given to child abuse situations. Nor did this workload split recognize the specific skill set required of community workers versus caseworkers. While social work education typically provides graduates with a range of generalist skills, casework experience does not automatically prepare a worker for the transition to community work, or vice versa. The skill sets and competencies required for community development work must be taken into consideration and we have already touched on the lack of attention to community work in schools of social work. Currently CAST community program staff are all full-time community work positions, with no case-carrying responsibility.

Funding full-time community workers within a child welfare budget also presents a significant challenge. In the beginning, the split workload was one way to validate the funding for these unique staff positions. For several years in the 1980s, the Program annually faced funding cuts. One year the funding situation for the Society was sufficiently grave that the Board of Directors slated the program for complete elimination. On each occasion, program staff called upon their organizing and advocacy skills to enlist sufficient community support to have the Society reverse its position. The recently introduced child-welfare funding formula in Ontario is presenting yet a new challenge for any non-protection, non-child-in-care related services currently provided by CAST. The Children's Aid Foundation, which funds child abuse and neglect prevention, has for the past few years funded a portion of the Community Work Program. Other sources of alternative funding may also have to be explored.

The survival of the Program is a significant achievement for the Society as a whole, for program staff, and for its community supporters. Agency support for the Program has probably never been stronger despite the significant reductions in funding and the stress CAST has experienced in the past several years. Agency leadership and commitment to prevention as a part of the spectrum of child welfare services is critical. But frontline support also is critical. It is understandable when frontline protection and children's services workers feel that caseload relief should take priority over maintaining a prevention service. An ongoing challenge for CAST's Community Work Program, therefore, has been to link community work activities with the needs of the children, youth, and families served by their protection and children's services colleagues. This can be a particular challenge if caseworkers have minimal awareness of or appreciation for the impact of public policy on their clients. In the current neo-liberal social, political, and economic climate, the impact of public policy and reduction in public spending to support children, youth, and families is all too visible, with an increasing number of children, youth, and families in distress. Over the past few years, the number of families receiving service from CAST has increased approximately 11 to 15 per cent, and the number of children in care has increased. Given these realities, frontline workers who daily work with more and more children and families have an appreciation for the social, political, and economic factors that create increased stress on vulnerable families.

Summary and Conclusions

We have explored here one community development program delivered within a child welfare setting. The availability of early intervention and primary prevention programs at the local community level is clearly in everyone's best interests. Supporting communities to assume responsibility for child neglect and abuse prevention is within the child welfare mandate. Bringing a child welfare perspective to broader public policy deliberations benefits all children, youth, and families and especially those served by child welfare. At the same time we have pointed to some particular challenges that appear to be rooted pretty firmly in the tradition of social work and social welfare which work against the likelihood that we will see any expansion of community work in child welfare. As well, the social and political milieu in Ontario, and indeed Canada, has rarely been less supportive of community action on issues of social justice. Part of this recent reality is a revised child welfare act that is less oriented to the prevention of conditions leading to the neglect and abuse of children and more focussed on the identification of "offending caregivers" and bureaucratic accountability. This context will provide a most severe challenge not only to the functioning of the community work program but to its survival.

On the other hand, as we have engaged in this examination we find that some of the factors provide an important ground for hope that community work can and will survive with the Children's Aid Society of Toronto. The following statement by Bruce Rivers, the Executive Director of the CAST, is a testimony to how it has proven its worth.

> For the past thirty years, the Community Development and Prevention Program has held a vital position on our child welfare service continuum. While it is relatively small the

workers have helped us to address the source of many of the problems that bring children and families to our attention in the first place. We feel that this is a remarkable program; its staff have been able to mobilize communities to take responsible action for their children and to organize around critical social issues such as child poverty, a lack of affordable housing and inadequate child care resources. The Program has helped to bridge our protection mandate, build lasting partnerships and strengthen community capacity to keep children safe.

notes

1. It should be noted that for the most part we are utilizing the term "community development" rather than "community organizing." This is because the CAST uses that term.

2. We would like to acknowledge the contributions of Mona Robinson, Mary Lewis, Lloyd Cooper, Don Bellamy, Gail Aikins, Glen Axle, and the current program staff.

3. For example, the Chetwynd Project, affiliated with a number of agencies, such as the CCAS of Toronto, works with disadvantaged communities in the Toronto area. It offers an essentially locality development approach in assisted housing communities. The London CAS mounted a CD program in the 1970s. The CAS in Guelph has a small program running at present. The CCAS of Toronto began a CD program in the 1970s, which lasted until provincial budget cuts in the mid 1990s. The York County Children's Aid Society maintained a small program from 1981 to 1989.

4. The CAST is a quasi-public agency. Its funding comes largely from the provincial government. It is mandated by, and operates under, provincial child welfare legislation. Like other CASs, it is managed by a board of directors composed of citizens elected at annual meetings of the society.

5. MacNevin chronicles her personal journey from abused wife and CAST client to community activist in her book *From the Edge: A Woman's Evolution from Abuse to Activism.*

references

Barr, D. 1971. "Doing Prevention," *Ontario Association of Children's Aid Society Journal* (Feb.).

———. 1979. "The Regent Park Community Service Unit: Partnership Can Work," in B. Wharf, ed., *Community Work in Canada*. Toronto: McClelland and Stewart.

Barr, D. and A. McLaughlin. 1975. "A Community Worker Prevention Program," *Ontario Association of Children's Aid Society Journal* (April).

Carniol, B. 1985. "Intervention with Communities," in S. Yelaja, ed., *An Introduction to Social Work Practice*. Scarborough: Prentice-Hall.

———. 1999. *Case Critical: Challenging Social Services in Canada*. 4th ed. Toronto: Between the Lines.

Children's Aid Society of Toronto. 1990. Mission and Value Statement.

———. 1991. Policy Statement (June 13).

———. 1993. Prevention and Child Welfare Policy Statement (6 Jan.)

———. 1997. Prevention Team Framework (May).

———. 1999. Annual Report.

Cross Branch Community Work Group. 1980. "Community Work in the CAS: A Framework for the 80s." *Report*.

Ife, J. 1998. *Rethinking Social Work*. Melbourne: Longmans.

———. 2000. "Localized Need and Globalized Economy: Bridging the Gap with Social Work Practice," "Social work and globalization," special issue of *Canadian Social Work* 2,1 (Summer) and *Canadian Social Work Review* 17, supplementary issue, *Intervention* 17: 50-64.

Jackson, S. and P. Nixon. 1999. "Family Conferences, A Challenge to the Old Order," in L. Dominelli, ed., *Community Approaches to Child Welfare: International Perspectives*. Aldershot, Hampshire: Ashgate Press, 117-46.

Lakeshore Area Multi Service Project. 1999. *Lakeshore Community Audit Project*. (March).

Lee, B. 1999a. *Pragmatics of Community Organizing*. 3rd ed. Mississauga: CommonAct Press.

———. 1999b. "A Community Approach to Child Welfare in Urban Canada," in L. Dominelli, ed., *Community Approaches to Child Welfare: International Perspectives*. Aldershot, Hampshire: Ashgate Press, 65-94.

Lee, B., S. McGrath, U. George, and K. Moffatt. 1997. "Community Practice Education in Canadian Schools of Social Work," *Canadian Social Work Review* 13, 2: 221-35.

———. 2000. "Defining Citizenship in Contemporary Community Work Practice," paper presented at the Joint Conference of the Canadian Association of Schools of Social Work and the International Federation of Social Workers, Montreal (1 Aug.).

Macintyre, E. 1993. "The Historical Context of Child Welfare in Canada," in B. Wharf, ed., *Rethinking Child Welfare in Canada.* Toronto: McClelland and Stewart.

MacNevin, W. 1999. *From the Edge: A Woman's Evolution from Abuse to Activism.* Toronto: Picas and Points Publishing.

McGrath, S., K. Moffatt, U. George, and B. Lee. 1999. "Community Capacity: The Emperor's New Clothes," *Canadian Review of Social Policy* 44: 9-23.

McKnight, J. 1995. *The Careless Society.* New York: Basic Books.

National Council of Welfare. 1998. "Child Benefits: Kids Are Still Hungry." Report.

———. 1999a. "Preschool Children: Promises to Keep." Report.

———. 1999b. "Children First." Pre-Budget Report.

Ralph, D., A. Regimbald, and N. St-Amand. 1997. *Open for Business, Closed to People.* Halifax: Fernwood Publishing.

Rothman, J. and J. Tropman. 1987. "Three Models of Community Organization Practice," in Cox et al., eds., *Strategies of community organization,* 3rd ed. Itasca, Illinois: F.E. Peacock Publishers.

Wharf, B. 1997. "Community Organization, Canadian Experiences," in B. Wharf and M. Clague, eds., *Community Organizing: Canadian Experiences.* Toronto: Oxford University Press, 1-14.

part three ————————————————————————————————

LEARNING FROM THE PAST / VISIONS FOR THE FUTURE:
THE BLACK COMMUNITY AND CHILD WELFARE IN NOVA
SCOTIA

CANDACE BERNARD AND WANDA THOMAS BERNARD

Introduction

This chapter presents a case study of the attempts of the Association of
Black Social Workers (ABSW) in Nova Scotia to change child welfare
services in order to meet the unique needs of Black[1] citizens in this
province. Interviews, documentary analysis, and a reflective analysis of
our own experiences with the organization were used to complete the
case study. We begin with a brief historical sketch of the African presence in Nova Scotia. This is followed by the case study of the ABSW.[2]
The chapter concludes with a discussion of lessons learned about community work and child welfare in the Black community and what we
hope to accomplish in the future.

African Nova Scotians: A Brief History

The first known presence of African people in Nova Scotia dates back
to 1605 (Pachai, 1990). Yet, it was at least 200 years before a significant number of Africans had settled in Nova Scotia. Africans found
their way to Nova Scotia through various entry points, including the
institution of slavery: as freed Black Loyalists, as Maroons from the
West Indies, and as refugees after the war of 1812 (Pachai,1990). Each
of these routes brought with it a different and significant history and
set of experiences, and all helped to develop what we now call African
Nova Scotian society.

The one experience linking each cohort of African settlers was the
stigma attached to the legacy of slavery, and the relegation of these settlers of African descent to the bottom of the hierarchy of Canadians
was common to all. This history of discrimination and inferiority based
on race is still evident today. Africans in Nova Scotia quickly learned
that free Blacks were not treated much differently from slaves. The
legacy of marginalization from the mainstream underpins contemporary issues of systemic racism and oppression. The "cycle of unequal
access" (Christensen, 1998) manifests itself in all sectors and segments
of society, including the child welfare system. That African Nova

116

Scotians survived as a distinct ethnocultural group is considered a miracle by today's activists (Hamilton, 2000; Pachai, 1990; Bernard and Bernard, 2000; Bristow et al., 1994). This survival is rooted in collective empowerment. A contemporary example of this collective empowerment can be found in the work of the ABSW.

The Association of Black Social Workers: The Formation and Structure of the Organization

The Association of Black Social Workers in Nova Scotia was established in 1979 as a professional, volunteer organization. The first ABSW in Canada was founded in Montreal in 1977. The ABSW in Canada is affiliated with the National Association of Black Social Workers in the United States, which began in San Francisco in 1969. ABSWs were formed throughout North America (primarily in the U.S.) and other parts of the world by social workers of African descent who wanted to raise concerns about the care African children were receiving from agencies run by the state. In Nova Scotia, the ABSW began with a small steering committee of four founding members.

The ABSW in Nova Scotia established the following goals to guide its development:

> To provide a structure and forum through which Black social workers and human service workers can exchange ideas, offer service and develop programs in the interest of the Black community and the community at large;

> To work in co-operation with, or to support, develop or sponsor community welfare projects and programs which will serve the interest of the Black community and the community at large;

> To examine, develop and support social work and community-based programs of direct service or assistance to individuals in the Black community. (ABSW, 1985)

The members of the ABSW are primarily African Nova Scotian social workers, social work students, and human service workers who work with the organization as volunteers in addition to their full-time employment. The ABSW acts as a support group for African Nova Scotian social workers, in addition to its function as an action-oriented community group. One of the first community welfare issues that the ABSW addressed was the provision of child welfare services to the African Nova Scotian community.

ABSW's Work and the Welfare of Black Children

In Nova Scotia during the late 1960s and early 1970s the trend in the provision of child welfare services moved towards foster homes and adoption placements for children in temporary and permanent care as opposed to placement in institutions such as the Nova Scotia Home for Colored Children (NSHCC), which had provided out-of-home care for Black children in need since 1917. Black children from across the province were no longer being referred to the NSHCC, sibling groups were not being placed there, families could no longer self-refer, and long-term stays were not being encouraged. As a result, there was a growing concern in the community about the significant number of African Nova Scotian children in care of the state but who were not being placed at the NSHCC. Many of these children were being placed in Euro-Canadian foster homes in isolated rural White communities. An ABSW member recalls some of the conditions.

> It was appalling. These kids were being raised in communities where they had no exposure to their racial heritage and no knowledge of their culture. They experienced so much racism. Many of them were forgotten by the agencies that had placed them. We wondered why they were not being placed at the NSHCC.

The programs developed by the ABSW have responded to needs in and demands by communities. A number of concerns were raised regarding the placement of African Nova Scotian children. Agencies were not actively recruiting African Nova Scotian foster and adoptive homes, despite the history of the helping tradition and "caring for our own" (Bernard and Bernard, 2000; Saunders, 1994). Moreover, Black and bi-racial children were being placed in Euro-Canadian homes without any cultural screening or cultural sensitivity training for these parents. This became a priority for the ABSW and a child-welfare placement committee was formed to facilitate advocacy and program development in this area. The various programs the ABSW has been involved with have evolved out of community need and a response to the community demand. The program discussed below linked youths living in isolated communities with other Black youth. Often a young person in foster care was the only Black person in the community.

ABSW Community Work

SUMMER PROGRAM FOR BLACK AND BI-RACIAL YOUTH IN CARE[3]

The Summer Program for Black and Bi-Racial Youth in Care was targeted for those youth who were living in white foster and adoptive homes. It was designed to help the youth deal with issues of identity, culture, and experiences with racism. The program linked these youth with each other and with other youth from the African Nova Scotian community. The majority of the youth who were referred to the summer program were living in isolated rural communities. In several cases a large number of Black and bi-racial foster children were living in one foster home. In one home there was a family of six, and in another, a family of five. The children were not related, but as the only Black children in the family and community they developed strong familial bonds. Most of these children experienced racism and a lack of cultural sensitivity in their homes, schools, and communities. Their foster or adoptive parents were not prepared or adequately trained to raise these children for the harsh realities they would face in a race-conscious and racist society (Bernard, 1996).

The ABSW Summer Program provided workshops for the youth on basic topics such as hair and skin care. There were also lessons in African Nova Scotian and world history, and sessions on building self-esteem and positive racial identity. The ABSW also provided seminars on dealing with racism and handling conflict.

An unanticipated outcome of the program was the fact that it reunited sibling groups. Youth who were separated when they went into foster care, and who were unaware of the fact that they actually had siblings, were suddenly in contact with them. In addition, the links with other community youth developed into ongoing friendships and in some cases long-term relationships. This linking of Black and bi-racial youth to their birth communities afforded them opportunities to build extended family and kin relationships that remain important ties for them today. An ABSW member recalls some of the experiences: "I remember one young woman who met her birth sister.... They were both amazed at the family resemblance. The sisters were so happy to have each other— it gave them the courage to look for their birth mother." Another says: "One of our participants met her future partner in that program. They are now very active foster parents in the community."

THE ABSW POSITION STATEMENT

The results of the program also had policy implications. Initially, it led the ABSW to develop a position statement regarding child welfare placements. The creation of a position statement about the placement of Black and bi-racial children in white foster and adoptive homes is one example of the ABSW's community advocacy in an effort to improve child welfare services. The ABSW stated that "the Black child should grow in a safe, secure environment with parents who are able to transmit to that child a positive sense of culture, identity, and well-being" (ABSW,1989). The statement also proclaimed that:

> The Association of Black social workers oppose the child welfare practices of transracial adoption and the foster placement of Black children in White homes. The Association of Black social workers adheres to the position that Black children be placed in Black homes where they belong physically, psychologically, and culturally in order that they receive a total sense of themselves and are free to develop to their fullest potential. In the adoption/fostering of a child of minority racial or minority ethnic heritage, in reviewing adoptive/foster placement, the court shall consider preference, and in determining an appropriate adoption/foster homes, the court shall give preferences, in the absence of good cause to the contrary to (a) a relative or relatives of the child, or if that would be detrimental to the child or a relative is not available, to (b) a family with the same racial or ethnic heritage as the child or if that is not feasible, to (c) a family of different racial or ethnic heritage from the child that is knowledgeable and appreciative of the child's racial or ethnic heritage and has ongoing contact with others of the child's ethnic or racial background. (ABSW, 1989)

This statement led to the active involvement of the ABSW in the development of the revised Children and Family Services Act in 1991 and to the inclusion as part of the Act of a policy on the provision of culturally specific services for children and families. The ABSW also assisted with cultural sensitivity and anti-racism training for staff of various child welfare agencies in the province as part of the implementation of the new Act.

The position statement and subsequent changes to the Nova Scotia Children and Family Services Act have made an important contribution to the provision of child welfare services in the province. Child-welfare workers and agencies now have the legislative responsibility to take racial and cultural issues into consideration when providing child welfare services, from the first point of entry in the system to service provision. Eleven years after the position statement was issued, workers continue to use it to make culturally specific case plans for Black and bi-racial children. The following comment from an ABSW member is illustrative of how the legislation is used to do more effective planning for cultural diversity in child welfare: "I was recently asked by a child welfare worker in a rural agency to do a consultation regarding placement options for a sibling group of four bi-racial children. I was impressed with the worker's strategy to build the consultation into the case planning for this family."

In addition to challenging child welfare agencies and criticizing their failure to locate Black foster and adoptive homes, the ABSW mounted an active recruitment campaign to help make implementation of the position statement and the new child welfare policy a reality.

RECRUITMENT OF BLACK FOSTER AND ADOPTIVE HOMES
The ABSW established a recruitment campaign to help agencies find suitable homes for Black and bi-racial children in care. A poster was prepared for use in the campaign and sent to strategic locations. In addition, ABSW members visited local churches and Black organizations to create awareness of the need for Black families to provide culturally specific foster and adoption options for these children.

This initiative led to the hiring of Black social workers in various agencies in Nova Scotia to recruit, train, and support Black foster and adoptive families. This work, however, is happening primarily in the urban areas and not in the rural areas of the province. Recruitment of Black foster and adoptive homes is a difficult task, as historically the African Nova Scotian community has not had a positive relationship with government agencies, particularly child welfare services. However, there is a long tradition of informal adoption in the African Nova Scotian community. The major task of the agencies and recruitment workers will be to bridge the historical interest in informal adoption with the current policies regarding fostering and adoption.

Anti-Racism and Cultural Sensitivity Training for Social Workers

As noted above, the ABSW has provided training in cultural sensitivity and anti-racism for social workers throughout Nova Scotia. This work was organized to assist social workers in developing culturally relevant services for the Black children and families in their care. The ABSW participates in the training of foster families, particularly around issues of race and racism. This early initiative led to the creation of anti-racism workshops for use in training of social workers, students, and human service workers. These workshops provide an interactive, intense simulation of racism that forces participants to examine critically their own power and privilege and to experience oppression first-hand during the exercise. The workshop has been integrated into the curriculum at the Maritime School of Social Work (MSSW) at Dalhousie University. The two-part workshop, which focuses on awareness, analysis, and action, is delivered by two ABSW members to the Introduction to Social Work class each year, and to students and faculty in a Masters of Social Work colloquium. The ABSW has also presented this workshop to over 50 agencies and organizations throughout Nova Scotia and other parts of Canada.

The Racism Awareness Workshop has been evaluated on two occasions; once by the ABSW itself and also by Kaireen Chaytor of Chaytor Educational Services. The goal in both of these evaluations was to examine the long-term impact of the training program. In each instance we learned that although participants were often angry and upset immediately after the simulation exercise, many described it as the single most significant learning experience they had around racism and anti-racism. The follow-up evaluations tracked students and practitioners who had participated in a workshop. Graduates of the MSSW state that "the ABSW exercise helped them to understand oppression far better than any reading, textbook or lecture." The experiential exercise touched them at the affective level and helped to provide the passion to engage in actions against racism in an ongoing way in their work and in their personal lives.

The ABSW has held three major conferences in conjunction with the Nova Scotia Association of Social Workers as part of its efforts to assist with the training of social workers: Preserving Black Families, Strengthening Resources for the Future (1989); Cultural Sensitivity in Social Work Practice with Black Clients (1990); and Africentric Perspectives in Social Work Practice (1997). Each of these conferences put the issues of Black families and communities squarely on the agenda of social work education, policy, and practice.

The ABSW has secured representation on the Nova Scotia Association of Social Workers Council. This enables us to work more collectively and collaboratively with all social workers in the province. In addition, it gives African Nova Scotians a voice, as the ABSW is able to bring critical issues affecting the community to the attention of social workers and to get support in dealing with these issues. In addition to the direct advocacy and community work with agencies, the ABSW has provided individual and group supports to community members who are involved with child welfare issues.

Support Groups

Two support groups were established by ABSW members, who were also graduate social work students. The first group was for Black and bi-racial adults who were raised in Euro-Canadian foster or adoption homes without a connection to their community of birth or their culture. Prior to the late 1970s there was little public discourse about transracial adoptions or foster care and much of the literature in this area focussed on the experiences of the parents, with little attention paid to the experiences of the children.

In 1989-90, an ABSW member conducted a qualitative study with Black adults on their experiences of being raised in white homes (Johnson, 1990). As they listened to others' stories in a focus group, the participants identified many shared experiences. This led to their interest in forming a support group. The support group was facilitated by the ABSW. The group enabled them to connect with each other and to support each other as they journeyed through the development of their racial consciousness. They went through a process of grief and a reclaiming of their identity. Eventually, the group members developed a strong and positive sense of themselves as people of African heritage, a heritage and culture that had been denied to them. The lessons learned from this group of adults who had survived transcultural placements were later used in training social workers. They also contributed to our understanding of the need to change child welfare policy to include issues of race, culture, religion, etc. in the provision of services.

The second support group, SEARCH (Support, Education, and Appreciation of Race, Culture and Heritage), was organized by another ABSW member and social work graduate student as part of her research on the development of identity in bi-racial children (Marsman, 1993).

The SEARCH group provided support, education, training, and counselling services for white parents who were raising Black and bi-racial children. The group included birth, foster, and adoptive parents, all of whom were mixed-race or Euro-Canadian couples or individuals (usually mothers), raising children of African heritage.

The SEARCH group enabled the parents to come together in a safe forum to address how best to meet the needs of their children. The group also provided opportunities for the youth to come together to address issues important to them. Many of the youth were dealing with issues of racism that they had not been able to discuss with their parents. In addition, the parents developed a heightened awareness and analysis of their role in effectively parenting their children to deal with the racism that they experienced. They also gained practical skills such as hair and skin care, how to access community resources, and the power of establishing networks in the community.

Besides these community-based group programs, the ABSW has also provided individual and family counselling and support and advocacy services to members of the African Nova Scotian community who requested assistance when dealing with various child welfare agencies. Initially, ABSW members provided these services as volunteers. However, this quickly proved to be an unmanageable service for volunteers. In addition, many of the members were employed by the state agencies, therefore their advocacy role with the ABSW often put them in direct conflict with their employers. A fee-for-service program was developed in 1995 to help fill this need for culturally relevant services for Black families.

Individual and Family Services

This program provides culturally specific services for African Nova Scotians involved with child welfare agencies as clients on a fee-for-service basis. The experiences of African Canadians in the child welfare and other social service systems, such as mental health, have been characterized by racism and poor treatment. Turner and Jones assert that "[t]he Black culture is sufficiently different from Euro-American culture, for misunderstanding of behavioural processes and functions to have occurred. This misunderstanding has resulted in problems in service delivery and treatment approaches." In addition, they state that "[B]lack patients are likely to evaluate therapy outcomes as negative if they feel that the therapist cannot understand them or their culture or is not interested in their welfare" (Turner and Jones, 1982: 21). Black practitioners are aware of this history and understand feelings of fear and animosity that may surface in the worker/client relationship. Because of the history of racist service in the past, many families will appreciate and may feel more comfortable having culturally specific services. Also, it can be frustrating for clients to have to educate workers about their race and culture.

Services provided by the ABSW include counselling, assessments, youth support work, tutoring, case aid, access visits, parent support, and advocacy work and are contracted with local child protection agencies. The ABSW has one staff person and one member of the executive who run the fee-for-service program. Skilled members of the African Nova Scotian community are hired by the ABSW to provide services on a contractual basis based on referrals from agencies.

The ABSW monitors the progress of the service providers through monthly reports and provides training to the workers. An evaluation of the program was carried out by a social work student at Dalhousie University as part of a field education placement. The student interviewed referring social workers from agencies, clients who have received services, and the fee-for-service workers. A major theme from the report, based on all of the interviews, was the appreciation of the culturally specific nature of the services. Regrettably, the number of referrals the ABSW receives has been reduced drastically over the past year and a half due to government budgetary restraints and a lack of awareness of the unique services provided. Furthermore, many agencies have not actively sought out culturally specific services, possibly because workers and administrators do not recognize the need or relevance for such services. The majority of the referrals for the fee-for-service program come from African Nova Scotian social workers in child welfare agencies. Many of the referrals are made when a case is at a crisis point, making ABSW interventions a challenge at best.

Although the fee-for-service program has received positive feedback from all of those who have used it (McNeil, 1997), the ABSW would like to see changes made to the program. This is the first major program the ABSW has delivered where there is a cost associated with the service. The ABSW often receives requests from individuals, agencies, and other community organizations for advocacy and other direct services on a volunteer basis. Of course, it would like to offer these services at no cost, as members have done in the past, and to community members who are not involved with protection agencies as prevention services. However, the ABSW's focus for prevention is based on broader structural issues, such as the role of race in custody and access decisions, as it does not have the resources to do individual case advocacy. It is impossible for ABSW members to meet this demand. Moreover, many ABSW members have experienced burnout, which makes it increasingly difficult to provide services on the limited amounts of grant funding it has received.

Future Plans

What is the best way forward for the ABSW? While some successes can be claimed, it is clear that with increasing demands on members' time and the increasing needs in the community, the existing volunteer model is no longer effective. Some ABSW members and other community members suggest that we should pursue a model similar to the First Nations communities, with a separate but state-funded social work agency for African Nova Scotians. Others prefer a structure where government would fund African Nova Scotian workers to provide social work services in the Black communities. Regardless of the model selected, the ABSW's present goal is to secure sustainable funding from government in an effort to meet the demands and need for child welfare services currently being offered at a cost to the African Nova Scotian community. As future directions are planned, the ABSW must consider a number of questions: Will government funding allow it to achieve its goals? Will it be in the best interests of the association and the community it serves? What type of trade-off will be involved? How would permanent funding change the direction and structure of the ABSW? Would the ABSW be able to remain grassroots? Are we willing to give up our autonomy to meet government regulations? These questions are particularly important for the ABSW to address if it pursues the model of becoming a social service organization.

While we are not in a position to answer these questions, we would posit that at this juncture in its evolution, the ABSW must ensure that it remains accountable and responsive to the African community. The grassroots nature of the organization has been integral to its survival. If the ABSW becomes a government-funded organization it would have to meet government regulations and expectations; however, the fundamental values and goals of the organization should not change if it is to remain accountable to the community. The ABSW formed to provide advocacy for the African Nova Scotian community, and it has especially emphasized on child welfare service provision since its inception. Advocacy and critique of provincial policies continue to be its first priorities. To remain grassroots, the ABSW must maintain its focus on community empowerment and advocacy. We can benefit from lessons learned from Mi'kmaq Family and Children's Services[4] and the Community Development and Prevention Program of the Children's Aid Society of Toronto,[5] both of which provide evidence of the ability to do community work in child welfare. Using an empowerment-based community development approach, the ABSW could have a more significant impact on the community if it had more resources. This is an obvious trade-off, as being state-funded would challenge the organization's autonomy. However, with a clear focus and a mandate to work with the community, and building on its proven track record, the ABSW could overcome these challenges.

There is also some recognition in government that it has a responsibility to better serve its Black citizens.[6] Clearly, there is a need for an African Nova Scotian presence within the provincial government. the ABSW has successfully developed a strong relationship with both the African Nova Scotian community and the larger mainstream social work community through its work over the past 21 years. We can build on these relationships as we move to become a state-funded organization with a mission to provide culturally relevant services to the Black community.

Children are considered one of the most valuable resources in African cultures (Bernard and Bernard, 2000). If the ABSW remains grounded in an Africentric[7] perspective in its provision of both micro- and macro-level services to the Black community, then the shift from being a volunteer group to becoming a state-funded agency becomes a less threatening issue. Meeting community need through research, policy, and program delivery would remain the core focus of the organization. With an emphasis on community capacity-building, as a state-funded group the ABSW could effectively work with Nova Scotia's Black communities to improve service provision and their access to existing services.

To conclude, the Association of Black Social Workers in Nova Scotia should be proud of its accomplishments. As a volunteer group it has had an impact on the community, and its activities and initiatives have helped to combat racism through both personal and institutional change. However, we are at a crossroads and change is inevitable. As previously noted, the small group of volunteers cannot possibly meet the social welfare needs of the Black community. Through these initiatives we have learned that the fight to eradicate racism must involve both perpetrators and survivors. We have learned to work in partnership with the social work community and the grassroots African Nova Scotian community. Perhaps the best way forward is to extend that partnership to include government in the efforts to change child welfare and other social services in order to meet the unique needs of Black citizens in Nova Scotia.

notes

1 We use the terms Black and African Nova Scotian interchangeably in this chapter.

2 Our interest in this work is both personal and professional. We are both members of the African Nova Scotian community and are active in the organization. Wanda is a founding member of ABSW, past president, former secretary, and co-ordinator of support services. Candace is a former volunteer and the first paid employee of ABSW, working part-time as Program Manager of the Fee-for-Service Program since 1997.

3 We use the term bi-racial to refer to children of dual heritage, in this case children of African and European ancestry.

4 See Gilroy (2000) for a discussion of the Mi'kmaq Family and Children's Services model of culturally specific program delivery.

5 See Chapter 4, Part II in this text, by Lee and Richards, for a more detailed discussion of the Toronto CAS community-based program.

6 In 1996, the Nova Scotia government-requested Task Force on Services to the Black Community reported that current services are inadequate, and there is a need to have more focussed attention within government to best meet the needs of the community. The task force recommended that this could best be accomplished with a Black secretariat with community development initiatives in each region of the province.

7 By Africentricity we mean the centering of the experiences of people of African descent. For a detailed discussion of Africentric theory see Bernard and Bernard (2000).

references

Association of Black Social Workers. 1985. "Aims and Goals," unpublished document. Halifax.

——. 1989. "Position Statement," unpublished document. Halifax.

Bernard, W.T., and C. Bernard. 2000. "It Takes A Village: Building Networks of Support for African Nova Scotian Families and Children," in M. Callahan, and S. Hessel, eds., *The Networking Approach to Child Welfare Practice*. Aldershot, Hampshire: Ashgate Press.

Bristow, P., D. Brand, L. Carty, A.P. Cooper, S. Hamilton and A. Shadd, eds. 1994. *We're Rooted Here and They Can't Pull Us Up: Essays in African Canadian Women's History*. Toronto, University of Toronto Press.

Gilroy, J. 1999. "Critical Issues in Child Welfare: Perspectives from the Field," in L. Dominelli, ed., Community Approaches to Child Welfare. Aldershot, Hampshire: Ashgate Press.

Hamilton, S. 2000. "African Baptist Women As Activists and Advocates in Adult Education in Nova Scotia," MA thesis, Dalhousie University.

Marsman, V. 1993. "The Identity of the Bi-Racial Child," MSW thesis, Dalhousie University.

McNeil, S. 1997. "The Association of Black Social Workers Fee for Service Program: An Evaluation," report submitted for Field Two credit, Maritime School of Social Work, Dalhousie University.

Pachai, B. 1990. *Beneath The Clouds of The Promised Land*, Vol II. Halifax: Black Educators Association of Nova Scotia.

Saunders, C. 1994. *Share and Care: The Story of the Nova Scotia Home For Colored Children*. Halifax: Nimbus Publishing.

Turner, S.M. and R.T. Jones, eds. 1982. *Behavior Modification in Black Populations: Psychological Issues and Empirical Findings*. New York: Plenum Press.

5

Community Control
of Child Welfare:

*Two Case Studies Of Child Welfare in First
Nation Communities*

part one

WATCHING OVER OUR FAMILIES: LALUM'UTUL' SMUN'EEM CHILD AND FAMILY SERVICES

LESLIE BROWN, LISE HADDOCK, AND MARGARET KOVACH

Introduction

There is no word in Hul'qumi'num, the language of the Cowichan people, for removal of children or child protection. Lalum'utul' Smun'eem means "Watching over, caring for our children, caring for our families and extended families." This name was chosen for the child and family services agency of the Cowichan tribes. It represents an important aspect of the agency's approach to the delivery of child and family services that the staff say is the moral of their development story—start with the community, start with the language of the community, and stay with the community.

The purpose of this chapter is to illustrate the unique challenges of providing child and family services within the context of a First Nations community. The Cowichan people have taken a strong community empowerment approach to the development and delivery of their child and family service system. Lalum'utul' Smun'eem Child and Family Services has made a commitment to community by stating that "We will work with the Community to serve the needs of the Community and will be open to listen and respond to the Community." This chapter will show how they have attempted to accomplish this goal and have explored the challenges of involving the community in a service that historically has been imposed upon them. Also included in this discussion are the implications of community-based child welfare practice. The findings reveal that integral to the operation of a First Nations child and family service agency is the task of managing the tensions that exist between a community empowerment approach to child and family services and the conventional child protection approach that dominates mainstream child welfare services.

According to elder teachings it is critical that worthy tasks are done in a "good way," which means respecting people and their culture and adhering to community protocols. When the authors began work on this paper, we felt it was important to start by following community protocol and inviting participation in a culturally appropriate way. Lise Haddock, the executive director of Lalum'utul' Smun'eem, was contacted and she in turn consulted the agency's Advisory Committee, which gave approval to proceed with the research and provided an elder to participate in a working group. We were fortunate to work with a group of individuals who carried out different roles within the agency. Lise Haddock clearly articulated the administrative and policy challenges that arise when working within a First Nations child and family service agency. The presence of Faye Griffith, the social worker, kept us grounded in the daily practice of child and family services, and Ramona Williams, elder, continually reminded us of the importance of culture and community values that underlie both policy and practice. We especially thank Ramona for providing guidance to our project.

The Lalum'utul' Smun'eem case study resulted from a series of conversations of the working group and the framework and analysis for the chapter evolved out of these conversations. Additional to the information arising from the interviews, we were provided with agency documents as contextual information. Each draft of this paper was reviewed and revised by the working group—a process with its own timing that was determined by the elder and our ability to "get it right," rather than by the publication timelines. Upon completion, the paper was presented to the Lalum'utul' Smun'eem Advisory Committee for their review and approval. This was an important step in recognizing their ownership of their experience and how it is presented to others.

The Vision and Services of Lalum'utul' Smun'eem

Critical to understanding the Lalum'utul' Smun'eem experience is appreciating the importance of the vision that guides the work:

> Cowichan Child and Family Services will promote a healthy Cowichan Community which supports everyone having a voice. With respect for tradition we will focus on our precious gifts of children, families, elders, and community. Cowichan Child and Family Services will work towards achieving this vision from a place of growth, equality, and strength.

This vision reflects the traditional values and beliefs of the Cowichan people. Children are sacred, and are the future of the Cowichan Nation. This vision has evolved from the premise that children have the right to be raised and cared for within their own community and that the Cowichan community knows what is best for their children. This means honouring the values of interdependency, relationship, and respect and placing in high regard the role of the extended family in caring for children. It is this vision, based on the values and beliefs of the community, which sets the standards of practice for the agency.

There are four types of programs offered by Lalum'utul' Smun'eem, including prevention, support, and child safety services as well as a special care home. A central component of Lalum'utul' Smun'eem services is the prevention programs, which evolved from generic services to specific programs aimed at addressing the needs of all children and families in the community. These programs included Kreative Kids Club (art therapy group); Growing Spirits (children in grief); Strong Children, Strong Families (children who witness violence); Healing in Relationship (women's group); and Summer Cultural Camps. An indication of the strength of the Lalum'utul' Smun'eem support program is the substantial increase in the number of foster homes since the agency's establishment. As a result they were able to develop a reciprocal arrangement with the B.C. Ministry for Children and Families (MCF) to provide Cowichan foster home placements for off-reserve Cowichan children. In addition, they have been able to open Hulithut, a community-based special care home for Cowichan children in need of protection. The term "special care home," rather than "group home," was chosen to reflect Cowichan values. Hulithut is based on a family care model rather than a staff model and is guided by the following vision:

> Hulithut is committed to being a Cowichan Community home for our children, in the spirit of healing and wellness. Our children will be met with respect for the strengths they bring to this safe haven. By providing guidance from our Elders, Community, and Family, Hulithut will recognize our Children as a sacred source.

The Child Safety Team provides services that include the assessment and response to reports on child safety, investigations of safety/protection concerns, and the placement of children in a safe environment if necessary. They also respond to on-reserve calls after hours that are reported to the Children's Helpline. The work of the Child Safety team is closely aligned with prevention and support services, such as parenting programs, in-home support, respite care, and referrals to counselling.

Lalum'utul' Smun'eem attempts to involve the community in its work in several ways. It offers community workshops, speaks regularly at community events, contributes to the Tribal newsletter and holds annual general meetings with the community. The advisory committee is active in liaison with the community and participates in several different inter-agency initiatives in the community (such as the Restorative Justice Project and the Residential School Project). In addition, Lalum'utul' Smun'eem has an open door philosophy and anyone can come in and chat about non-case-specific issues. Being visible in the community and generating awareness of the programs offered is an ongoing challenge for Lalum'utul' Smun'eem.

Context and History

The Cowichan are situated in the southern region of Vancouver Island, near Duncan, B.C., and comprise the largest First Nation community in British Columbia, with a population of approximately 3,500 people, of which 50 per cent live on the reserve. A chief and council govern the Cowichan tribes. The tribes offer a variety of programs and services to community members, including Lalum'utul' Smun'eem. The community (including the families, youth, elders) and the community leaders have been key players in the successful development and ongoing functioning of child and family services in this community.

EARLY DAYS

The initiative to develop a child and family service agency (initially called Khowutzun Child and Family Services) began in the 1970s in response to several growing concerns. The community was becoming aware of the increasing number of child sexual abuse disclosures, teen suicides in their community, and the growing number of Cowichan children in the care of the Ministry of Social Services (now known as Ministry for Children and Families). They were also concerned that the ministry removed their children without any consultation with the community, and given a lack of Cowichan foster home placements, children were placed in white foster homes often at some distance away.

In these early days the social development program was responsible for implementing preventive health services, including child and family programs, but as the momentum for developing a community-based child and family service agency grew, a child welfare committee was established. This committee took on the responsibility of developing a child and family services agency. It started by developing a number of community support services to attend to the prevention of child sexual abuse and teen suicide, and in 1976 hired professional social workers to act as liaison with the local ministry office. The Child Welfare Committee felt it was critical to develop a working relationship between their staff and the local ministry social workers in order to have some influence in the case planning for their children in the care of the ministry. During this time, whenever the ministry apprehended a Cowichan child, a Cowichan social worker was contacted. This was significant in several ways—the community became involved in the practice relating to their children, and both the local ministry office and the Cowichan community grew accustomed to Cowichan representation in child welfare matters.

"There was a desire [by the community] to see Cowichan children and families served professionally by Cowichan people, and there was also a wish to have Cowichan people more aware of their rights, and more aware of helping one another with family problems (Lannon, 1999: 4)." This process began with Project Child, a community-driven project that responded to child sexual abuse. Politicians from the band and from the local Friendship Centre increased their awareness of child sexual abuse through their involvement in Project Child. By the late 1980s the Cowichan leadership was giving voice to key child welfare issues and in 1988 a Band Council resolution was passed to decry abuse and to commit to the provision of services to children and families through a delegated model of service delivery. This resolution was a catalyst for support of the transfer of child and family services and signified the readiness of the Cowichan for this move. Shortly thereafter, in 1989, the tribes developed a funding proposal, which they submitted to the Department of Indian and Northern Affairs (INAC), to plan for the development of a child and family service agency. While simultaneously planning with INAC, the tribes were negotiating with the provincial government in preparation for the transfer of authority. All was ready when INAC, that same year, declared a funding moratorium on the development of First Nations child welfare agencies.

During the INAC moratorium the Child Welfare Committee continued to prepare the community, and when the moratorium was lifted in 1991 the Cowichan tribes received INAC funding for the pre-planning and planning phase of a child and family service agency. The tribes hired consultants, who worked in conjunction with the Child Welfare Committee, to carry out the pre-planning and planning tasks. The planning group implemented a four-part strategy to engage the community, which included:

- four large community meetings to keep the community aware of the process and progress in developing the new agency;

- workshops to educate community people on the role, function, and services of the agency;

- a community needs assessment, which used the information that had been accumulated by the Child Welfare Planning Committee over the past years; and,

- one-on-one communication between tribal staff and community members.

DELEGATION

By January 1993, a Delegation Enabling Agreement was signed between Cowichan tribes and the B.C. Ministry of Social Services for the provision of voluntary services for families—the new program was called Khowutzun Child and Family Services. In 1993 the Child Welfare Committee completed its work and over the next three years there was a gradual transfer of child welfare authority to the Cowichan. The tribes increased their delegated authority incrementally, beginning with the voluntary services as a first level of delegation, then in 1995 taking on a second level of delegation, which included the recruitment and retention of foster care homes.

However, as the Khowutzun Child and Family Services neared its second level of delegation, significant upheaval was occurring in the Ministry of Social Services. New child and family service legislation was being developed concurrent with an inquiry into the death of a young boy, Matthew Veaudreuill, known to the ministry. The inquiry, carried out by Judge Thomas Gove in 1995, resulted in major changes to ministry structure and standards. During this period the Khowutzun child and family service program evolved into an agency and in 1995 received a new name—Lalum'utul' Smun'eem Child and Family Service Agency. To provide guidance and direction to the new agency, an Advisory Committee was struck. Chief- and council-appointed representatives to the Committee and the general membership elected community representatives, including elders and youth. In 1996 Lalum'utul' Smun'eem acquired "full delegation," which included the full range of services from prevention to the protection of children.

The community hosted a traditional ceremony to acknowledge the full delegation responsibilities of Lalum'utul' Smun'eem. The ceremony took place in the Somena Big House and was witnessed by the community. It was an opportunity to publicly establish the relationship between Lalum'utul' Smun'eem, the community, and the ministry and it helped to clarify the role of Lalum'utul' Smun'eem to the Cowichan people. Ministry officials were wrapped in traditional blankets and escorted into the Big House for a ceremony that included a children's dance and a traditional mask dance. Holding a traditional ceremony demonstrated that the delegation did not belong to the ministry, but to the Cowichan community.

Shortly thereafter, new legislation, the Child, Family and Community Services Act, was proclaimed. The combination of changes brought about by the new legislation and the Gove Report unleashed a series of changes to the ministry that reverberated from its highest level of bureaucracy to the social workers on the front line. The general mood was unsettled, and the relationship between the ministry and Lalum'utul' Smun'eem was impacted by the tension. Also, this new legislation required that the existing Delegation Enabling Agreement between the B.C. government and the Cowichan tribes be renegotiated to reflect the new statutory requirements. To date, this has not yet been accomplished and reflects the difficult relationship between the provincial government and Lalum'utul' Smun'eem.

Concurrent to maintaining a relationship with the ministry, Lalum'utul' Smun'eem also had the task of maintaining accountability to the community. In 1999, the Cowichan commissioned an evaluation of Lalum'utul' Smun'eem, which resulted in a comprehensive review of the community's response to the agency's effectiveness. It captured the voices of elders, youth, foster parents, children in care, council members, and the general Cowichan community and found that:

- people appreciate that the social workers are Cowichan or from other First Nations;

- Lalum'utul' Smun'eem is more understanding and supportive than MCF; and,

- the foster training and support services offered by Lalum'utul' Smun'eem are a great strength.

The review also identified that Lalum'utul' Smun'eem should pursue the delivery of off-reserve services to Cowichan children and families. Provincial and federal support would be required to realize this goal.

AUTHORITY AND FUNDING

While the legislative authority Lalum'utul' Smun'eem receives to carry out child protection services is delegated, it attempts to deliver services, wherever possible, in a manner consistent with cultural autonomy. The ministry and its staff espouse respect for such a stance, but their actions and attitudes often suggest that First Nation's service delivery approach is secondary to that of the ministry. The integration of the computer systems is a good illustration of this contradiction. In its early days, Lalum'utul' Smun'eem could not access the ministry's case management computer system. Eventually, MCF provided a computer to access the central database but it could be accessed only through an MCF worker stationed in their office. It was not long thereafter that the computer was "apprehended" from Lalum'utul' Smun'eem. Feelings of frustration accompanying these events prompted the agency to develop its own comprehensive information system. Several other First Nations agencies have followed suit. While there is a need, recognized by both the province and First Nations agencies, for the various systems to be able to share information with each other, the debate centres on how. The ministry wants its system as the central hub with First Nations child and family service agencies connecting to it. Lalum'utul' Smun'eem would like the ministry to be treated as one agency in a group of many, with no agency in the centre but with all having the capacity to interface with one another. Lalum'utul' Smun'eem is maintaining a strong stance, as this is symbolic of the autonomous relationship that First Nations agencies want with the ministry.

Equal to the struggle for agency autonomy is the challenge of obtaining adequate funding to provide effective services. INAC currently funds the operations and maintenance costs of a First Nations child and family service agency through a funding policy known as Directive 20-1. This directive outlines four developmental stages that groups are required to fulfill before its services can become fully operational. Funding is available to assist groups to move through the stages. While the directive acknowledges the importance of gaining community approval for the development of a child and family service agency (which is demonstrated through a Band Council resolution), very little funding is available for groups to engage in community development activities. The need to invest in the community is critical and there needs to be monetary recognition of the importance of community in developing and maintaining services, including preventive programs.

Directive 20-1 provides maintenance funding to agencies based on the number of children in care, as per the Child, Family and Community Services Act. A child or family must be assessed as in need of services before funds begin to flow. "Maintenance costs are reimbursed monthly based on claims made by agencies to DIAND [federal Department of Indian Affairs and Northern Development] for the actual costs of keeping children in foster homes, group homes and institutional facilities" (AFN, 2000: 88). Unfortunately, the kind of services that can be included in maintenance costs are not clearly defined, and as a result the type and range of preventive services that an agency can offer is limited. One recommendation put forth by a committee reviewing Directive 20-1 "would be to define maintenance and its corresponding funding method, which could be directly linked to provincial legislation, policies and standards" (AFN, 2000: 91). This would ensure that First Nations children, many of whom live in remote areas, would have access to services comparable to those available to non-First Nations children. Many First Nations communities do not have on-site services such as community-based psychologists, speech therapists, and specialized residential resources that currently are not defined under maintenance costs.

Restrictions on jurisdiction and funding impact the ability of Lalum'utul' Smun'eem to be fully autonomous, and create an inherent contradiction between a community empowerment approach and a delegated model of child and family service practice. The computer system scenario is symbolic of the ministry's desire to be at the centre of the flow of information, as is the imposition of an external, centralized child welfare legislation and practice on First Nations agencies. This is indicative of a major power imbalance and points to the neocolonialism embedded in delegated child welfare models. It is the resistance to a prescribed model that will carve a new path for the delegated agencies. "There are no relations of power without resistances: the latter are all the more real and effective because they are formed right at the point where relations of power are exercised" (Foucault, cited in Wade, 1995: 178). The ability of Lalum'utul' Smun'eem to exercise choice in the way it carries out its services is a strength and a powerful statement about community empowerment.

PROFESSIONALIZATION
The key to community control of child welfare is to have Cowichan people delivering services to Cowichan children and families. This raises the question of the current link between professional credentials and the ability to practise social work in First Nations communities in B.C. In order for a First Nations agency to be able to receive fully delegated authority for child welfare services, 75 per cent of the workers employed by the agency must have a BSW or the equivalent (Ministry for Children and Families, 1999). This standard is applied without any critical review of the appropriateness of BSW education to child and family services in First Nations communities. The concept of "professional" is still grounded in the Western educational and practice experience—an ethnocentric assumption about the right way to do things. Professionalization represents a system of standards and credentials that does not recognize Cowichan workers with 20 years of community practice experience but no professional degree. The standards are supported by the academic structure of the majority Euro-Canadian society rather than by the community structure of the Cowichan people. Even in university programs with Aboriginal social work content, the institutional framework and non-Aboriginal concept of social work education limit the cultural authenticity of such programs. While Lalum'utul' Smun'eem has been able to employ First Nations people with degrees, not all have been Cowichan people. The requirements of professionalism impede efforts to build community capacity and do not facilitate the integration of Cowichan ways of knowing and working.

Another illustration of the impact of professionalization is the treatment of elders who act as a resource to social workers and children in

care. Other resource people, like psychiatrists and mental health workers, are considered professionals and are paid for their services. Elders,
however, may perform just as important a service to children, and therefore deserve to be compensated at a rate equal to a Western-educated
professional. Another issue to consider is that elders have traditionally
been used in the community as a resource for children. This is part of
the important role they play. What does it mean to compensate them
with money for something that traditionally has been their responsibility? How does money professionalize elders as a resource? The
involvement of elders in the work of child and family services, both at
an individual level (i.e., working with children and families) and at an
organizational level, is one of the distinguishing features of Lalum'utul'
Smun'eem and other First Nations community approaches to child and
family services.

Building capacity through education and training is recognized as
important to Lalum'utul' Smun'eem. Grounding that education in the
community and in the culture is important to ensuring that a Cowichan
community approach to child and family services is not lost. Valuing
the different kinds of knowledge and expertise is critical to effective
community empowerment work.

ALL CHILDREN ARE THE MANDATE

Lalum'utul' Smun'eem sees itself as caring for all Cowichan children
and families, not just those children at risk or taken into care. The
agency takes a holistic view of its mandate, rather than using the defi-
ciency model that characterizes most mainstream agencies. The agency
strives to attain a positive approach that supports all families. The community activities are illustrative of this approach. For example, Lalum'utul'
Smun'eem holds an annual child's day where all families attend, and
offers a range of preventive programming that is open to any family in
the community. This approach changes the nature of the practice of
social workers. When one is concerned with the well-being of all people
in the community rather than just the children in care or at risk of
coming into care, the work has to include community development,
health promotion, and other aspects of generalist practice.

As the mandate is the community, not just some children or families, maintaining a dialogue with the community is part of the work.
Lalum'utul' Smun'eem holds workshops and other activities to maintain an ongoing relationship with the community. This dialogue with
the community is not a regular feature of mainstream approaches to
child welfare. Yet it is consistent with the values of community caring

for children. As noted in the Lalum'utul' Smun'eem values, relationships are important and therefore tending relationships between the agency and the community members is part of the work.

Lalum'utul' Smun'eem is a young organization and yet has taken a long time to develop. As an elder said, "it takes a long time to do it well." While it has worked hard to incorporate the community in its work, there is agreement that this essential factor remains an ongoing emphasis. If they had to do it over again they agree they would work even harder to engage and prepare the community.

The Practice

The strength of Lalum'utul' Smun'eem agency practice is the underlying premise that knowing who someone is and where he or she comes from is important. The agency workers know the child, the family, the extended family, and the history of that child and family. This comes from the shared experience of living in the same community and is not the type of information that would appear in a child's file. It includes a general understanding of the impact of issues such as residential school, family violence, and substance abuse on a client's family. Knowledge of the family also includes having information about family members who participate in community activities, in culture, in healing, and so forth. Lalum'utul' Smun'eem workers have access to information about their clients through informal (i.e., going to bingo, attending feasts) as well as formal processes. They have to be mindful of unique confidentiality issues that arise when working in their community and have to be careful about what knowledge they use in making decisions about children and families. They also have to be aware that the community monitors how they use community knowledge in their professional work.

Lalum'utul' Smun'eem believes that people have the ability and the right to heal. The breadth of knowledge workers have leads to different kinds of decision making than is possible by the Ministry for Children and Families. For example, Faye Griffith has been a social worker in the community for 20 years. She knows clients from when they were children and knows their history, not from a file but from having a relationship with them and their family. A composite client profile of "Susie" typifies the vulnerabilities and strengths of many Lalum'utul' Smun'eem clients. Several years ago, Susie was a chronic alcoholic living on the streets of Vancouver. Today, she is back in the community participating in substance abuse programs and is beginning to make healthier decisions in her life. Her children are in care of Lalum'utul'

Smun'eem and the challenge for Faye is whether to base a decision regarding the continuing care of her children on the past or on her potential. This is a practice dilemma and the question arises: what do workers give weight to? Faye knows Susie's mom, knew Susie when she was little, knows her brothers and sisters, and knows what supports she has around her. Faye's decision, then, is not based only on Susie in isolation, but on the strength of her family to support her and/or her children. There exists the possibility to place Susie's children in temporary care with extended family, while supporting Susie in healthy choices and working towards the reunification of Susie and her children. The approach means that the worker must know the history and context of Susie's life situation and must put in the time to work with both Susie and her family.

This approach to practice stands in direct contrast to the deficit approach to child welfare practice which is fostered by the legislation, and practice tools such as the risk assessment model. Increasingly, child welfare decisions in the Ministry for Children and Families are determined by these practice tools which tend to numerically assess and evaluate the risk and vulnerabilities of clients without necessarily knowing much about their support systems and strengths. In addition, Lalum'utul' Smun'eem is fortunate that it is not encumbered by large caseloads that necessitate the "drive-through" approach to child welfare practice that many front-line workers from MCF are currently faced with in B.C.

It is Lalum'utul' Smun'eem's experience that community-based practice is less intrusive than that of the ministry as the children can stay within the community regardless of their in-care status. This minimizes the trauma associated with separation and placement of children. They can attend their school, activities, and family functions regardless of residence. Also, continuity of care for children and families is enhanced by the fact that the social work staff at Lalum'utul' Smun'eem tend to stay. Out of 12 positions, only four social workers have left over the six-year life of the agency, and one of those has since returned.

If residents of the Cowichan community were asked to name Faye's title they would not be able to do so. At the ministry, individual and team titles are important because a client has to know the titles in order to access the services. At Lalum'utul' Smun'eem, staff are known as people. A client would ask for Faye, not for the Co-ordinator of Support Services. Although there are distinct departments in Lalum'utul' Smun'eem, the work is shared. Therefore a client, regardless of the issue, could access services through any worker. Social workers are seen as community members, as well as social workers, and often clients drop by rather than make appointments. In addition, the community doesn't operate from 8:30 to 4:30 and therefore social workers make themselves available outside normal office hours. It is important to the agency that they not develop an elaborate bureaucracy and that they maintain easy entry for clients. Clients don't drop in to visit ministry social workers; they do so at Lalum'utul' Smun'eem.

Another illustration of the relationship between Lalum'utul' Smun'eem and the community is the client complaint process. In the ministry, clients watch videos and read pamphlets to uncover the mysteries of the procedures of the complaint process. In Lalum'utul' Smun'eem, they march from Faye's office to Lise's office and ask that the problem be fixed. As one five-year-old said to Lise, "you work for me." And he is right. When Lalum'utul' Smun'eem began, rarely did families approach with complaints. Today, they not only express their complaints but also expect them to be worked out.

Is Lalum'utul' Smun'eem Working?

In combination with the other self-determination initiatives, such as the Health Centre, the Cowichan community is much healthier than it was a decade ago. Indicators of this success take several forms. Before Lalum'utul' Smun'eem began, alcohol abuse and family violence were community norms. Today, while it continues to be a problem for some families, it is the exception rather than the norm. Children are being immunized and there is more awareness of health promotion and disease prevention, and there has been an expansion of programs and services. Children who come to Lalum'utul' Smun'eem are happy, playful, assertive, and well-taken-care-of. There are waiting lists of children who want to get into Lalum'utul' Smun'eem programming, and off-reserve families are requesting the assistance of Lalum'utul' Smun'eem workers or want to access the agency's programs. There is a substantial increase in the numbers of people who come to Lalum'utul' Smun'eem asking for help, rather than waiting for intervention. People now make complaints where they didn't before. While in the same period, the number of off-reserve Cowichan children taken into care by the ministry has increased markedly, the average number of on-reserve children in the care of Lalum'utul' Smun'eem has remained stable.

Discussion

In the course of our conversations with our working group, it became clear that three constructs impact the Lalum'utul' Smun'eem agency: delegation, community empowerment and self-conscious traditionalism. The findings of our discussion revealed the inherent contradictions of delivering child and family services in a First Nations community through a delegated model of service delivery.

DELEGATION

The question that emerges from a delegation model is whether the use of external tools and processes will bring the First Nations agencies closer to the goal of community self-determination or create a further gap. An executive director of a First Nations agency clearly articulated this dilemma when he stated, "all problems must be solved within the context of the culture—otherwise you are just creating another form of assimilation" (Squires in Bruyere, 1999).

Lalum'utul' Smun'eem's experience with the ministry has been a double-edged sword. The early positive relationship between the tribes and the ministry facilitated the delegation of authority, and when the ministry seconded a social worker to Lalum'utul' Smun'eem, the agency had control of who would be seconded and for how long. Despite these precautions, the presence of the ministry social worker was as much a challenge as a benefit. This position brought with it the ministry perspectives, values, and beliefs and the Cowichan staff were concerned about this philosophy influencing their agency. Cowichan workers also were vulnerable to developing a dependency on the ministry social worker in that they could do the prevention and family support work but could rely on the ministry workers to do the apprehension work. It became clear to Lalum'utul' Smun'eem and the entire community that an important part of taking on the authority for child and family services meant taking on the responsibility of apprehension when it was required.

It was important to Lalum'utul' Smun'eem that the notion of community accountability be stressed. "Accountability in the indigenous sense needs to be understood as not just a set of processes but as a relationship" (Alfred, 1999: 91). The elder in our working group told us that part of the early work was determining how to set up the agency according to the cultural values. The values that underpin Lalum'utul' Smun'eem continue to frame the relationship with the community. While the relationship with the community is fundamental, the delegation model of child and family services demands that agencies like Lalum'utul' Smun'eem are primarily accountable to the Director of Child Protection. Under the Child, Family and Community Services Act the Director is responsible for the protection of children in the province and holds guardianship responsibility for children in care of the ministry. This includes children taken into care by agencies with delegated authority from the province. The task of Lalum'utul' Smun'eem is to balance accountability to the community and to the Director—an unenviable position of serving two very different constituents. The history of many First Nations communities (including Cowichan) with the government has been marinated in years of distrust. It is not surprising that the community may have qualms about a delegated model. This form of centralized accountability has not been effective in solving child welfare problems in First Nations communities historically (Gray-Withers, 1997: 92).

The basic premise that children must be protected and given the opportunity to thrive is a shared view of the Lalum'utul' Smun'eem and the ministry. How this basic premise is carried out can often be a source of conflict between First Nations communities and the ministry. This dual accountability is a constant strain on the autonomy of the Cowichan tribes and on the daily practice of Lalum'utul' Smun'eem social workers. It is here that the straightforward principle—Cowichan people know what is best for Cowichan children—gets tested time and again.

Neo-colonialism refers to colonialism that is still present in many activities, policies, and programs that are being delivered in First Nations communities, but are designed and formulated by the mainstream. Colonialism, like the trickster, can change shape according to its environment and its time. The mask of today's colonialism is painted with subtle colours and is covered in the veil of empowerment and a just society.

The delegation model is based in neo-colonialism. It is founded on the notion of "giving" authority to deliver child welfare services, rather than recognizing First Nations' inherent authority to care for their children. Further, it imposes a way of thinking about and practicing child and family services that is based on mainstream concepts, beliefs, and practices. While delegation allows for some adaptation to accommodate culture and promote community empowerment, it doesn't challenge the fundamental beliefs that construct concepts of child protection. Is delegation wrong? Not entirely. It provides a mechanism for community empowerment. It ensures that there are Cowichan people involved in the administration and delivery of child and family service practice in their community, and this is a huge improvement. However, it is a mechanism that maintains, rather than relinquishes, power and control. It is about working inside a box constructed by someone else.

The dualities and tensions that face First Nations child and family service agencies reflect the complexity of the relationship between Aboriginal peoples and the state. While interdependence exists within the relationship, it is still based upon two different value systems and this creates contradictions. Because of the colonial relationship, however, the work of managing the dualities that arise (such as dual accountability) are left for First Nations people to handle. The work of child and family services in a First Nations agency is, therefore, larger and more complex than that found in non-First Nations communities.

COMMUNITY EMPOWERMENT

Community empowerment is a model of practice that simply means people know what is best for their own communities. This approach is based on the assumption that people are able to identify their needs and the services required to address those needs. Solutions to community problems must come from the community, not be offered by well-meaning outsiders. This is particularly true of First Nations communities because of the distinct cultural contexts. Too often in the past, and continuing into the present, First Nations have been offered programs and services built upon cultural values alien to their communities. We do not have to look further than previous attempts by mainstream social work to impose child welfare programs on First Nations peoples, causing trauma and damage to children, families, and communities. If a program is to be beneficial to First Nations, or at minimum honours the notion of "do no harm," it must originate in the community.

Lee describes community empowerment as follows: "[A]s we begin to strive for the accomplishment of one or more of the objectives—as we find that we can participate in a discussion or that by making our voices heard we begin to be listened to—we are developing a sense that we have the ability to influence our lives" (Lee, 1999: 68). He points to the link between individual empowerment and community empowerment. In First Nations communities this is particularly salient as the healing of First Nations people is inextricably linked to the capacity of the community to exercise their rights of self-determination.

Community empowerment is a strong theme in the work of Lalum'utul' Smun'eem. Their goal is to care for their children. The values that guide their work are based in notions of community, relationships, and accountability. Lalum'utul' Smun'eem notes in its vision that it "will promote a healthy Cowichan Community which supports everyone having a voice." This began with the early community consultations around what the child and family services program should look like. It has consistently asked for community feedback through an open door policy, evaluations, and the ongoing dialogue with the community. This dialogue is not a regular feature of mainstream approaches to child and family services, but is consistent with the values of community caring for children.

McKenzie (1999: 211) suggests three outcome-oriented measures for assessing community empowerment. These measures include "the extent to which the community exercises a constructive influence concerning agency services and programs, the level of partnership arrangements between child and family services and other programs on community-building initiatives, and the degree to which the community is proactive in dealing with issues such as abuse or the need for prevention." The extent to which the agency can actualize these objectives is largely established by the nature of the relationship with the state. This encompasses not only the structural relationship between Lalum'utul' Smun'eem and the province, but also the working relationship between Lalum'utul' Smun'eem social workers and the local MCF social workers. Depending upon their nature, relationships can be helpful to community empowerment or can be a barrier. For many First Nations agencies, including Lalum'utul' Smun'eem, the relationship with the MCF largely depends upon the latter's ability to recognize that there can be differing paths to the same destination.

Accountability within the community also needs to be highlighted, as it is a hallmark of a community approach to the delivery and practice of child and family services. A strong and clearly articulated relationship between politicians and the agency is important to maintain credibility, accountability, and responsibility for practice. There is a strong commitment from the community leadership to Lalum'utul' Smun'eem and its work. The dialogue between the leaders and the staff of Lalum'utul' Smun'eem is active and daily. Yet, the roles and relationship are clearly defined to ensure that while the agency is accountable to the leadership (and community), political interference in practice is unacceptable.

Further, as can be found in many small communities, the practice of social workers is very transparent to the community. This makes the accountability of the worker to the community immediate and real. Workers have to have built relationships within the community in order for trust to inform their practice. The community can call the agency to account for their practice. The collective philosophy of the community can include historical and cultural practices, not only the standards as outlined in formal written standards of practice. It is the community's active participation in the operation of the agency that makes it community-based, and it is Lalum'utul' Smun'eem's ability and desire to respond to community guidance that makes the experience empowering.

SELF-CONSCIOUS TRADITIONALISM

"Self-conscious traditionalism" is the process of identifying traditional values and consciously using them to inform contemporary activities. Alfred (1999) coined this term to describe how the re-adoption of traditional values is central to decolonization as it entails "adopting patterns of thought and action that reject colonial premises." In short, it means consciously thinking about how to apply traditional values here and now. For Lalum'utul' Smun'eem, that means taking the Cowichan values rooted in tradition and consciously exploring ways to use them in the daily practice of child and family services. These values are not just traditional in the sense that they reflect practices of long ago; they find contemporary meaning as they inform the organization, delivery, and practice of "watching over, caring for our children, caring for our families and extended families" (Lalum'utul' Smun'eem).

The elders play an important role in self-conscious traditionalism. The concept of elders as teachers who are valued for their life experiences is central to First Nations cultures. The importance of elders is a result of generations of First Nations people holding firm to the traditional value that elders must play a specific and key role in the community. We have elders today, as a culture, because we have collectively and self-consciously affirmed their role. By their very presence, elders remind the community of the commitment to traditional values and the importance of self-conscious traditionalism. This we must not lose.

In Lalum'utul' Smun'eem, elders are involved at an individual level (i.e., working with children and families) and at an organizational level. The elders remind the workers, the community, and the agency to always pay attention, to consciously incorporate Cowichan values of respect, interdependency, and the sacredness of children in their work. Extended families are another example of a traditional concept that is useful to present-day child welfare practice. Lalum'utul' Smun'eem relies on extended families in the caring for children. This includes extended family being involved in discussions of care plans for children, potential placements for children, and the monitoring of children's well-being. The role of the extended family is an illustration of self-conscious traditionalism within the community. It not only challenges colonial notions of what "family" is and what is best for children, but also enhances community empowerment through validating the culture. When Lalum'utul' Smun'eem articulated in its vision statement the importance of Cowichan values in the delivery of child and family services, it was continuing the important work of self-conscious traditionalism.

Consciously having the community as the construct that frames the practice is central to doing the work in a traditional way. A community approach to child welfare practice for Lalum'utul' Smun'eem means a cultural, a Cowichan approach to caring for children.

The hope of the delegated model is in the resistance activities of First Nations. This resistance work is critical, as MCF will not relinquish control on its own. The stance that Lalum'utul' Smun'eem has taken on the seconded MCF worker and the computer system are two examples of resistance, of asserting control. It is about shaking off colonialism—for First Nations it is about reclaiming authority, for MCF it is about goodwill and the ability to let go. The struggle to maintain self-conscious traditionalism in the face of a delegated model of child and family services defines the resistance, and here lies the heart of community empowerment.

Speaking out about issues, such as the contradictions that arise from working within a First Nations delegation model of child and family service, is also resistance work. It is seen as a responsibility to our children. As Lise noted, "If we stay silent, then we're teaching our kids to be silent."

references ───────────────────────────

Alfred, Taiaiake. 1999. Peace, Power, Righteousness: An Indigenous Manifesto. Toronto: Oxford University Press.

Assembly of First Nations (AFN). 2000. "First Nations Child and Family Services, Joint National Policy Review, Draft Final Report."

Bruyere, G. 1999. "Empowerment," in Aboriginal Social Work Training Project—Curriculum. Victoria: Caring for First Nations Children Society.

Gray-Withers, D. 1997. "Decentralized Social Services and Self-Government: Challenges for First Nations," in J. Pulkingham and G. Ternowetsky, eds., Child and Family Policies: Struggles, Strategies and Options. Halifax: Fernwood Publishing.

Lannon, V. 1999. "Hwu'kwam'kwum–Getting Stronger": An evaluation of Lalum'utul' Smun'eem.

Lee, B. 1999. "A Community Approach to Urban Child Welfare in Canada," in L. Dominelli, ed., Community Approaches to Child Welfare: International Perspectives. Aldershot, Hampshire: Ashgate Press.

McKenzie, B. 1999. "Empowerment in First Nations Child and Family Services: A Community Building Process," in W. Shera and L. Wells, eds., Empowerment Practice in Social Work: Developing Conceptual Foundations. Toronto: Canadian Scholars' Press.

Ministry for Children and Families, Province of British Columbia. 1999. Aboriginal Operational Practice Standards and Indicators. Victoria.

Wade, A. 1995. "Resistance Knowledge: Therapy with Aboriginal Persons Who Have Experienced Violence," in P. Stephenson et al., eds., Canadian Western Geographical Series 31: A Persistent Spirit: Towards Understanding Aboriginal Health in British Columbia. Victoria: University of Victoria: Western Geographical Press.

part two ─────────────────────────────────────

BUILDING COMMUNITY IN WEST REGION CHILD AND FAMILY SERVICES

BRAD MCKENZIE

Introduction

Community organization is not new to First Nations communities. It was first launched as a federal government initiative in the 1960s (Young, 2000). However, that program largely reflected the policies of assimilation in that its primary goal was to stimulate economic development initiatives borrowed from dominant society. Community work within a social development framework in Aboriginal communities has a more recent history, yet dates back at least three decades. For example, a community organizing approach was associated with the development of a locally controlled Child Care Centre in Sandy Bay, Saskatchewan, in the early 1970s (Pawson and Russell, 1985). This initiative, designed to prevent the placement of children in non-Aboriginal child-care facilities outside the community, was developed long before the devolution of child welfare services to Aboriginal communities.

The devolution of child welfare services to First Nations communities has resulted in a new emphasis on prevention and early intervention and these functions often have been associated with a community organizing approach within these agencies. Despite the principled commitment to local resource development and community-based services, successful implementation has often been affected by limited resources, an inability to use existing financial resources in a more flexible way to promote such initiatives, and the level of skills among local staff. At the same time there have been a number of important community-based initiatives in Aboriginal child and family services. This particular case study was selected because it represents an approach that evolved following the devolution of control over child welfare services to a First Nations agency where governance involves a form of local community control. As well, it was felt important to examine an agency with a significant history in implementing a community-oriented approach. In the case of West Region Child and Family Services (CFS), community organization was incorporated as a specific program when the agency first received its child welfare mandate in 1985. In addition, the agency's philosophy of service emphasizes a community-based approach.

Data from this case study were gathered during a comprehensive review of agency programs and services completed in 1999. The study (see McKenzie, 1999) involved a wide range of interviews, a survey of local Child and Family Service Committee members, document study, and observation of the agency's planning processes. Information was subsequently reviewed by agency staff for accuracy. Consultation with the agency's Executive Co-ordinator captured more recent changes.[1]

Agency Context

West Region CFS has provided a full range of child welfare services to nine First Nations communities in western Manitoba since 1985. While the agency provides regionally based specialized services for child abuse investigations and alternate (i.e., foster) care, it has developed a very decentralized community-based service model over the past several years. Each locally based service team has staff designated as child protection workers, prevention and resource development workers (community organizers), and treatment support staff (who provide more therapeutic and support services to individuals and groups). A locally based supervisor exists in larger communities, and in smaller communities a supervisor may be responsible for local workers in more than one community. Each community has a well-developed Child and Family Services (CFS) Committee composed of community volunteers who meet regularly with staff and play key roles in planning and decision-making. Careful attention to service quality has been reinforced by an emphasis on professional training for staff, as well as training programs for child welfare committee members and foster care providers.

Agency operations are guided by a mission and vision statement based on the teachings of the medicine wheel, and values based on respect, responsibility, authority, and accountability. The vision statement also emphasizes the agency as an extension of the kinship system where "everyone—elders, leaders, grandmothers, grandfathers, mothers, fathers, aunts, uncles, sisters, brothers, husbands, wives—is an advocate for children and families." Core values stress the importance of the following: preserving families and communities; the incorporation of traditional values and teachings in the programs and services provided; and the right of First Nations to self-determination and full jurisdiction over child and family services to all members of the tribal council living both on and off reserve. The agency articulates a philosophical commitment to the provision of holistic, community-based services that focus on healing individuals, families, and communities, and this principle is frequently identified as a guide to service and program planning.

In 1992, the agency negotiated a block funding arrangement for child maintenance costs with the federal government as a pilot project. This arrangement, the first of its kind for First Nations child welfare agencies, has been renewed on an annual basis since that time. Under block funding the agency can use funds, normally paid out only as per diem costs for children in care, to both meet the needs of these children and launch new resource development and family support initiatives. For example, funds that might normally be paid to a residential treatment facility in Winnipeg only after a child had been placed in this resource can be used to develop more culturally appropriate resources in West Region communities. While surplus funds can be carried forward for a reasonable period of time, deficits are not recoverable unless circumstances arise that are beyond the agency's ability to control. While the funding arrangement is limited to services funded by the federal government, this represents the largest proportion of the agency's overall budget for child maintenance. In 1998 the agency was the recipient of the Peter T. Drucker Award for Canadian Non-Profit Innovation for its use of block funding and the medicine wheel framework in service development.

Community Organization and Community-Based Services

The agency's service model is based on its mission and value statements, and there has been a consistent emphasis on the development of community-based services and the use of a community organization process to program development. For example, in a unique approach to community-based planning, regional operational workshops, involving all staff and a wide range of representatives from each community, are held every two years to review agency programs and provide input to future plans. In addition, each community-based team holds a community planning workshop annually or every two years to identify local service and program priorities. Not only is this a form of community accountability, but it also serves as a vehicle for setting priorities, community education, and the recruitment of community volunteers willing to assist in implementation. Thus, it becomes one element in a more general strategy aimed at building a community-wide philosophy of caring. This approach to community planning is consistent with the developmental process used in establishing new resources and programs. For example, staff who undertake resource development initiatives began with a needs and capacity assessment phase. These activities include the active participation of community groups in the planning and implementation phase of project development.

Community-building initiatives that involve the development of new resources have been facilitated by the flexibility afforded in the block funding arrangement. One initiative has been to develop a therapeutic foster home program and a related training program that includes content on culture and identity. Another initiative has focused on the development of more specialized resources for youth with greater needs. Miikanaa Centre provides culturally appropriate residential treatment services for adolescent males who have sexually offended or are at risk of doing so, and Oshki-ikwe, a facility with 10 furnished suites, provides residential prenatal and postnatal programs for adolescent mothers. The development of local resources for high-needs adolescents keeps these children closer to home and reinforces community responsibility for caring. In addition, more culturally appropriate interventions can be designed, and the teachings of the medicine wheel are used in the planning and delivery of services within these facilities.

Three other examples demonstrate the use of a holistic community approach to program development. One is the initiation of the Vision Seekers Program, a partnership program designed to develop life skills and educational upgrading for youth. Using financial resources from several sources, the agency hired community facilitators to undertake a circle consultation process with youth and other members to discuss how the program should operate. The consultation phase has generated a great deal of interest and the project has now entered the program design and implementation phase. A second is the agency's leadership role in the development and operation of the Mino-Bimaadizi Project ("To lead a good life"). This project, developed through a partnership arrangement with Chief and Council in one community, provided life skills, computer training, and related support services for 20 young parents with children in care or at risk of coming into care. Third, a developmental approach has been used to establish a community-based response to problems associated with fetal alcohol syndrome and effects (FAS/E) based on the teachings of the medicine wheel. The agency's response to FAS/E issues can be sharply contrasted with the medical model, which stresses a diagnostic approach to the problem, often leaving parents with an overwhelming sense of guilt and few instructions on how to respond. Instead, the agency's Children with Special Needs Co-ordinator has spent time providing information and education, and building a network of parents who can both provide support to each other as well as help to support a broader community response to this important issue.

The agency's primary investment in community organization is reflected in its continuing commitment to the placement of community organization staff (called prevention and resource development or PRS workers) within each locally based team. Some of these staff are enrolled in the distance-education BSW program, or have a BSW degree, and some have other forms of training. All have a close connection with the local community. These staff have primary responsibility for the planning and implementation of outreach and prevention services, although they also provide backup protection services on an emergency basis. An additional responsibility is the co-ordination of early intervention services that involve homemakers and family support workers, although the direct employment of "case aides" has reduced the demand for short term family support workers.

Programs reflecting the early intervention and prevention mandate include education and support programs, the promotion of community healing through traditional teachings, and the development of workshops and group programs to address identified community needs. For example, sharing and healing circles to address issues pertaining to family violence and FAS/E are sponsored, and programs related to parenting, male violence, and cultural awareness for youth are organized. Cultural camps, suicide prevention programs, and parenting programs are but some of the initiatives organized by local community workers.

One of the purposes of the alternate programs is to provide resources that can support families and children where child protection is a concern. Yet participation is not limited to those who may be receiving child protection services from the agency, and this avoids the stigma so often associated with programs targeted at "problem families."

These programs are developed through a process best described as community-building. Local CFS Committees participate with community workers in developing an annual service plan with a specific focus on prevention and resource development. Expenditures related to proposed activities are then estimated and these plans are referred to a regional committee that includes at least one representative from each community. Local priorities are approved based on established agency goals and priorities as well as budgetary considerations. An approved community prevention plan, along with the budget allocation, is then provided to each local CFS Committee, and the Committee and community work staff are then responsible for implementation and accountability. While this process reinforces the need for community planning and accountability, there is sufficient flexibility to allow community workers to respond to new needs or priorities that emerge during the course of the year. Direct expenditures for these community-based programs increased almost threefold over the five years between 1994 and 1999.

Assessing Effectiveness

One perspective on the scope of the agency's investment in community-based prevention and resource development is gained by comparing the rate of staff resources devoted to community organization and resource development initiatives and those devoted to other child welfare functions performed by the agency. Seventeen, or 27 per cent, of the 63 professional staff employed as direct services staff or special development co-ordinators are involved in community work or new program development initiatives. One can also examine expenditures for child maintenance devoted to children in care and the amount used for alternate forms of community programs. In 1999-2000, approximately 68 per cent of the child maintenance allocation was spent on services for children in care, whereas 32 per cent of the block grant was spent on alternative programs that focused on resource development, community-building, and early intervention.

Despite the investment in alternate programming, this does not occur at the expense of child protection services. For example, service quality reviews by the province have indicated that agency compliance with service standards has been above average. This is consistent with the balanced holistic approach to child and family espoused by the agency where protecting children, supporting families, and building community capacity become part of the circle. Attention to child protection is reinforced by a community-oriented model of services, which includes a CFS Committee in each community that has received training in child welfare. Leadership in these committees is most often provided by respected women in the communities and they are actively engaged in both child protection and prevention programs. On child protection matters they meet regularly with local staff and provide advice and assistance, including active participation in family conferences, as appropriate. Because of the active involvement of community members, the provision of child protection services reflects a more consultative, collaborative approach with the community than that found in conventional child welfare agencies.

While it is difficult to quantify the effects of this more integrated approach to community work and community-building, there is no doubt that it has led to the development of more culturally appropriate resources for children closer to home. For example, 75 per cent of all placements of children in care in 1998 were made to resources where there was at least one Aboriginal caregiver, almost half of all placements were within the child's own community, and 44 per cent of all paid care days were with extended family members. By comparison, only about 23 per cent of the children formerly from West Region communities who were taken into care in Winnipeg were placed in culturally appropriate resources. It has also facilitated the development of culturally based programming both within these new resources and as a component of community outreach. Some positive effects on placement prevention and costs for children in care are apparent. For example, the rate of federal funding for children in care in West Region Child and Family Services over a five-year period declined from 7.3 per cent to 5.5 per cent of the child population in these communities. This rate was significantly below a comparison agency that as yet has been unable to implement a sustained community-building program. In addition, per diem costs for children in care in 1999 were below the provincial average and 17 per cent below the average costs paid in the city of Winnipeg. Block funding has enabled increased investment in community-building activities, and agency forecasts suggest that the termination of block funding and the range of community-based programs it supports would lead to a significant increase in children in care and related expenditures targeted specifically for these children.

While placement prevention and costs are important reasons for supporting community work and community-based services, the real measure of success is found in indicators of child, family, and community well-being. Although program initiatives earlier described are highly valued and there is anecdotal support for their effectiveness, more evaluation of the effectiveness of community prevention programs is required. Nevertheless, one indication is provided in the responses of local Child and Family Service Committee members to a survey on perceived changes in service delivery. When compared with four to five years ago, respondents "agreed somewhat" that the community was dealing more effectively with child welfare issues now and that child and family services had improved.

Discussion and Implications

At the local community level, community organization in West Region CFS reflects a locality development focus where the emphasis is on strengthening community capacity and promoting community-based early intervention and healing initiatives. While all staff may initiate advocacy activities on behalf of an individual or family, group or system advocacy efforts receive more limited attention at the local level. In part this may reflect the training and skills of community workers, but it is also determined by local politics and current practices in the agency. For example, it is more likely that group advocacy actions, directed at either local or external systems, would be undertaken as an institutional response and carried forward by senior management.

Major resource development initiatives that have implications for the entire agency are often launched by staff with designated responsibility for these initiatives. While they become resource development "specialists" who incorporate a social planning approach, they work collaboratively with other staff and local community members.

The agency has made a conscious effort both to integrate a community-building philosophy into its operations and to promote community organization through staff with designated responsibilities for such activities. The integration of a community-building philosophy is reflected in the emphasis on community-based services. This community-oriented, developmental approach is an attempt to wrest child welfare services away from its history based on colonization to a future based on empowerment. In many respects this transformation is consistent with the philosophy and approach associated with the "patch" program in the United Kingdom (Hadley and Young, 1990), which was developed in an effort to create more responsive community-based public services. In an Aboriginal context, this includes an emphasis on traditional values and practices that support a community approach to caring and a more holistic approach to practice. In small but practical ways this includes linking developmental goals with child protection functions. For example, in one community, women with children at risk are enrolled in a parenting program open to all women where both social support and group activities are promoted. Younger children are placed in daycare; thus, the program provides both respite and opportunities for learning. One parent with six children who was receiving protection-oriented services described the program this way: "Child and family services has saved my life. They are the only ones that listen to me and this is the only place I feel safe."

A community-oriented approach to child and family services in First Nations communities is also driven by necessity in that new resources and programs must be developed if the political goal of self-determination in child and family services is to have any real meaning. And while it may be easier to establish an integrated community-oriented approach in a smaller or medium-sized Aboriginal agency, many other Aboriginal agencies have been less successful in this endeavour. Three factors appear to be important to some of the successes experienced by West Region CFS. One is the availability of resources to enable alternate investment in community-building. A second is the strength, commitment, and consistency of agency leadership to this model of practice. And a third is the willingness to invest in skill development and training to facilitate this model of practice.

Generic skills and knowledge are important to effective practice, and some of these were being acquired by staff through participation in the distance-education BSW and MSW programs offered through the University of Manitoba. However, other qualities were also regarded as important. One was a strong commitment to the agency's service orientation and its developmental approach to practice. Second was the knowledge and ability to integrate traditional cultural practices, as appropriate, in new programs and initiatives. Third was the ability to establish collaborative, respectful working relationships with community members. Two additional qualities were identified as important for staff members working in their community of origin. These were the ability to manage demands from community members, including family members, and a perspective on personal healing that enables them to respond appropriately to friends and neighbours experiencing personal problems.

While the extent to which a community organization philosophy and approach guide agency operations is encouraging, challenges remain. First, additional knowledge and skills for community workers could expand the scope and effectiveness of their activities. For example, there is the potential to develop a more co-ordinated service response by allied service providers within local communities, and the range of advocacy services could be expanded in some communities.

Second, as the agency decentralizes by giving more responsibilities to local communities, there is a risk that community-building initiatives may be replaced by other priorities set by local community decision-makers. In some cases these decisions can reflect an intolerance for diverging patterns of behaviours or narrowly defined political priorities, a problem described by Montgomery (1979) as "acute localitis." Other potential risks include a tendency for governments to support decentralization as a means of offloading responsibilities. From an agency perspective inefficiencies in program management can occur if all child and family service functions are decentralized to each community, particularly where communities are quite small. While these risks need to be recognized, they are reduced by an investment in training for both staff and local volunteers, and by the demonstrated success of a community-building approach to child welfare practice. In this regard, evaluation of new and emerging approaches to the delivery of child and family services in First Nations communities can play an important role. For example, it has been generally demonstrated that social supports, including access to community resources, mutual aid groups, and supportive social networks, are associated with improved parenting (Cameron, 1995; Fuchs, 1995), but the specific characteristics and effects of programs that work in First Nations communities require more attention. Two other policy initiatives may be important to this issue. One is the development of a more coherent body of service standards for Aboriginal child and family services, and an accountability structure that will provide support in meeting culturally appropriate standards. The recent initiative of the province to extend Aboriginal control over child welfare services to those living off-reserve may encourage more attention to this. A second is the potential benefits in efficiency and effectiveness that may be realized through the integration of child and family services with other community-based human services. West Region CFS has demonstrated that new resources and a more co-ordinated community response can be developed in partnership with other formal and informal groups and organizations, and this could evolve into a more formalized single unit service delivery structure.

A "resource gap" is particularly apparent in First Nations and other Aboriginal communities because there is an absence of voluntary organizations and services that often play an important role in developing a variety of family and children's programs to supplement the formal child welfare system. In Aboriginal communities, community partnerships are possible, but they are more likely to involve a relatively small group of other publicly funded service providers and community members. In this context, First Nations child and family service agencies must have the capacity to invest more financial and human resources in community social work than those child welfare agencies that operate in a richer social resource environment. In this regard, block funding of child maintenance costs can provide some opportunities for alternate investment if funding levels meet the criterion of adequacy. Block funding arrangements have been established with a few First Nations agencies across the country, but the federal government has not yet established a policy that would make this option more widely available. Such a policy will need to address criteria for establishing the level of the block grant, a formula for ongoing adjustment and factors that affect the agency's capacity to utilize the grant both to meet the required needs of children and families and to build community capacity.

note

1. The author wishes to acknowledge all staff and community members who so willingly shared their views on service development in the agency and in their communities.

references

Cameron, G. 1995. "The Nature and Effectiveness of Parent Mutual Aid Organizations in Child Welfare," in J. Hudson and B. Galaway, eds., Child Welfare in Canada: Research and Policy Implications. Toronto: Thompson Educational Publishing, 66-90

Fuchs, D. 1995. "Preserving and Strengthening Families and Protecting Children: Social Network Intervention, A Balanced Approach to the Prevention of Child Maltreatment," in J. Hudson and B. Galaway, eds., Child Welfare in Canada: Research and Policy Implications. Toronto: Thompson Educational Publishing, 113-122

Hadley, R., and K. Young. 1990. Creating a Responsible Public Service. New York: Harvester Wheatsheaf.

McKenzie, B. 1999. Evaluation of the Pilot Project on Block Funding for Child Maintenance in West Region Child and Family Services: A Second look (Final Report). Winnipeg: Child and Family Services Research Group, University of Manitoba.

Montgomery, J. 1979. "The Populist Front in Rural Development: Or Shall We Eliminate Bureaucracies and Get on with the Job?," Public Administration Review (Jan./Feb.): 58-65.

Pawson, G., and T. Russell. 1985. "The Practice of Community Work in Child Welfare," in S.H. Taylor and R.W. Roberts, eds., Theory and Practice in Social Work. New York: Columbia University Press, 353-87.

Young, D. 2000. "The Historical Development of Indian Welfare Policy in the Prairies, 1940-1967," MSW thesis, University of Manitoba.

6

Searching for Common Ground:

Family Resource Programs and Child Welfare

JANICE MACAULAY

As Chapter 3 made clear, many good things can happen when child welfare agencies and community-based programs work together. Case studies in this book and elsewhere (Schorr, 1997) describe efforts by child welfare services to embrace the principles and practices of community work and to collaborate with community groups to improve services and outcomes for families. However, even when support for these initiatives has come from senior levels within government and the child welfare sector, the inherent differences between traditional child welfare services and community-based services present significant barriers that require determination on both sides if they are to be overcome.

Community-based family resource programs currently offer a wide range of supportive programs and services to families that are involved (or potentially involved) with child welfare agencies. Although congenial working relationships between child welfare agencies and family resource programs certainly exist in some communities, many family resource programs have described their interactions with child welfare as problematic. This chapter will explore some sources of tension that exist between these two services, identify a number of common problems that arise and suggest some ideas for building bridges at the community level with the aim of serving families and children better. It is based on the findings of a project undertaken by the Canadian Association of Family Resource Programs (FRP Canada) on behalf of its member programs and in partnership with the Canadian Institute of Child Health and the Child Welfare League of Canada. The project objectives were to encourage a productive dialogue between family resource programs and child welfare services in their communities and to increase the capacity of family resource programs to work with families considered at risk of child abuse and neglect. The research involved nationwide consultation with family resource program staff, child protection staff, parents, and others, and was funded by the Population Health Fund of Health Canada.[1]

What Are Family Resource Programs?

Over the past 25 years, family resource programs have emerged from their grassroots beginnings to become a model of choice for service delivery. With their user-friendly approach and ability to meet families "where they're at," family resource programs currently reach hundreds of thousands of families each year across Canada.

Family resource programs are defined as much by their approach to working with families as by the program components they deliver.

> They strive to work in a holistic way that takes into account the systemic and interdependent nature of families' lives and the way families and their members are affected by the communities in which they live. Family resource programs are also characterized by their conscious attention to family support principles, which focus on prevention and the promotion of well-being, and they seek to foster individual, family and community strengths. Through advocating with or on behalf of families, and actively taking part in or facilitating local social planning and community development efforts, family resource programs work to strengthen community life. (Kyle and Kellerman, 1998: 55)

The effectiveness of family resource programs as a model of service delivery is challenging to measure, in part because there are such great differences between them. Services are multi-faceted, focused on the whole family, and change over time. In Canada, some large-scale evaluations of community-based programs for families have been undertaken—the national and regional evaluations of federal Community Action Programs for Children projects and the first stage of a longitudinal evaluation of Better Beginnings, Better Futures projects in Ontario.[2]

Preventing child abuse and neglect

These words—first from a parent who attends a family resource program (Sullivan, 1999: 34) and then from family resource program staff members—suggest that timely and appropriate supports can turn things around dramatically for families that are under stress.

> Without this centre I don't think my family would still be together. It was pretty rocky before we came. But now we deal with things differently, see different ways to do things and my mind is more open now. I can't really explain it. If you knew us, you'd really see that there is a difference now.

> The act of child protection is often not a colossal event but a series of small events. Until the Big Kaboom happens, there is little or no attention given to the family. Once the Big Kaboom happens, you realize that the Big Kaboom didn't have to happen at all.

> Have supports when it's needed, not when it fits into a time slot. It's having the care when it's needed, when they're reaching out. And when they're reaching out, that's when you have to reach them—today. Not Monday or even next Monday.[3]

Practitioners in the family resource field believe that child abuse is associated with preventable factors such as poverty, family history of poor parenting, and isolation. Through the provision of a range of supports, family resource programs strive to ameliorate these negative influences and strengthen family functioning, thus reducing the need for involvement with the child welfare system. However, family resource programs report that they are now working with more families that are involved at the same time with child welfare agencies, and that working relationships between themselves and child welfare agencies are often far from satisfactory.

In response to a question on the project questionnaire, a family resource program practitioner summarized the way she saw the situation:

> Child welfare agencies are in crisis and we witness the chaos daily and how it affects families. Individual child protection workers are struggling to deliver best practices but are not able to. FRPs are viewed as services that could be another "arm" to provide interventions to "clients," and we resist that to ensure that our relationship with families is volun-

tary and trusting. The two models—medical/deficit-based and FRP and community supports—don't interface well.

Similarities and Differences

An appreciation of the influences that shape and define family resource programs and child welfare services is necessary for understanding some of the day-to-day difficulties. Both groups share a belief in the importance of children's well-being and the role of families in keeping children healthy and safe. Furthermore, both experience the ongoing frustration of having to stretch inadequate resources to fulfil their mandates. The backgrounds and qualifications of staff members may be quite alike.

Despite these similarities, many structural and philosophical differences exist between these services, and it is not surprising that tensions and misunderstandings result. It should be noted that the comparison below is based on a generalization of the two sectors and that accordingly the precise reality will vary somewhat from community to community.

AUTHORITY

Family resource programs operate with the authority of the communities they serve. Often, members of these communities have worked hard to establish these centres and fought hard to maintain them. Through the involvement and support of citizens as voluntary participants, helpers, and board members, family resource programs demonstrate their legitimacy. The authority of child protection agencies, on the other hand, is founded in provincial or territorial legislation, and these organizations operate with the force and power of law.

MANDATE

Whereas family resource programs engage primarily in health promotion and prevention activities with families and communities, child welfare agencies typically intervene after a concern about child abuse or neglect has been raised. The mandate to protect children from harm commands tremendous respect in our society, and day-to-day family support activities may appear to be somewhat trivial in comparison. In many provincial/territorial jurisdictions, the prevention activities of child welfare agencies have been scaled back considerably due to funding constraints and a greater emphasis on child protection. This has put added pressure on non-profit organizations in the community to fill the gap.

PRINCIPLES AND PRACTICE: "IT'S NOT WHAT YOU DO, IT'S HOW YOU DO IT."

Family resource programs seek to build on family strengths rather than on deficits or problems.

When you show families that you believe in them and that they have strengths, they start to believe in themselves. Then you can have change.

> If you have the belief that a person can change their circumstances, if you give them the supports to do that, that's very different than "you're all screwed up and I'm here to help you."

Relationships with participants are based on mutual respect and trust. The focus is on the whole family, and programs are frequently aimed at parents and other adults. "If mom's okay, then the kids are okay."

As well, "services are holistic and not narrowly targeted and thus do not stigmatize or alienate individuals or groups with special needs. We see parents as partners, we do not refer to them as clients" (Kyle and Kellerman, 1998: 28). Family resource programs believe that all families, not only those labelled "at risk," should have access to supportive programs. With a few exceptions, programs are voluntary and open to all. A sense of ownership by program participants is encouraged, and parents and other community representatives serve on boards of directors. Participants are routinely invited to give feedback and are encouraged to be involved in formal evaluations of services (Ellis, 1998). Most family resource programs keep very limited contact data on participants, and some keep no records at all, since they believe it is not their function to evaluate or report on their participants' involvement in program activities.

Flowing from their mandate to protect children from harm, staff in child welfare agencies routinely deal with very serious situations involving families in crisis. When assessing risk, they must answer the question: "How bad is it?" Families are identified first in terms of their problems. Relationships with families are formal and carefully documented; client status is often described as "having a file open." Unless a file is open, services generally are not provided. The child is the primary focus of intervention, and the needs of the other family members are assigned less importance.

STAFF BACKGROUND, QUALIFICATIONS, AND TRAINING

Employees of family resource programs bring a wide range of backgrounds and qualifications to their work. Applicants typically come to the field as a later career, and their backgrounds may include early childhood education and child care, social sciences, social work, nursing, parenthood, and volunteer work. Life experience and "people skills" are frequently considered as important as formal qualifications when hiring decisions are made, and staff members are often recruited from the community served by the program. This means that qualifications are unpredictable and include both professional and non-professional credentials (Kellerman and MacAulay, 1998). Although this diversity enriches the field greatly, it may be misunderstood or undervalued by those outside the field.

A university social work degree is the qualification most sought by child welfare agencies, which often look to new graduates—who may be young, childless, and inexperienced—to fill the ranks as child protection workers. A recent newspaper advertisement for "frontline workers" for a large urban child welfare agency makes a deliberate effort to recruit graduates who will thrive and prevail in combative situations. The ad seeks "heroes" who have "courage, nobility, and strength" and "the 'Right Stuff'" to join "this elite group." They should possess a "passion for excitement" and "enjoy the rush" of responding to crises (*Globe and Mail*, 2000). Although many child welfare workers would not be comfortable describing themselves in these terms, the commonalities between workers (similar educational backgrounds, extensive in-service training, and tough day-to-day experiences) contribute to the formation of a strong professional identity. This can create a barrier to collaboration with family support workers in the community, who may be seen as well-meaning but not highly qualified and perhaps somewhat naïve. Family resource program staff frequently report that their experience and abilities are not recognized by child welfare social workers.

We are treated as less educated and less knowledgeable.

We changed our job titles to be heard. The position was renamed Parent-Child Counsellor rather than Nursery Worker.

I feel I have to use my title and parade my degree to get any respect as a professional.

ORGANIZATIONAL CLIMATE AND STRUCTURE

Most family resource program practitioners enjoy egalitarian, supportive work environments within small to medium organizations. Creativity and flexibility are hallmarks of this sector, and organizations can be reconfigured fairly easily in response to changing needs. Work brings the daily reward of building stronger families and communities. Despite modest pay scales, job satisfaction generally appears to be high, and practitioners often stay in the field for many years.

In contrast, child welfare organizations typically are large, bureaucratic and hierarchical, with clear status distinctions between first-line workers and supervisors. Change happens slowly, and is imposed from the top. Daily work is often very stressful and crisis-related, and sometimes it involves risks to personal safety. Relationships with clients are often strained. Staff turnover in many agencies is very high, so that young and inexperienced workers are frequently expected to deal with very complex and difficult situations.

FACILITIES

Family resource programs typically are located within the heart of communities and may be found in settings as diverse as church basements, schools, houses, community centres, non-profit housing developments, and shopping malls. With modest, accessible locations and home-like furnishings, family resource programs are friendly and welcoming spaces where both adults and children can move about freely, relax, and enjoy themselves.

Generally, the facilities of a child welfare agency are more formal. Parents may approach appointments at these offices with dread and recall them later with feelings of anger or shame. Parent-child supervised visits frequently take place in small rooms furnished with a few toys, two-way mirrors, and closed doors. These visits are unnatural, tense situations where everyone's behaviour is closely monitored and evaluated. Child welfare offices can become associated in the minds of clients and others in the community with powerlessness and discouragement. In some communities, child welfare agencies have made arrangements with family resource programs to use community space for meetings between child welfare workers and parents, for supervised visits or for parent groups.

ACCOUNTABILITY AND LIABILITY

Family resource programs are accountable to their participants, their boards, their communities, and their funders. Child welfare agencies are accountable to the courts and to the government department or board under which they operate, as well as to the children they are mandated to protect, the other family members, foster parents, and the general public. Consequences of mistakes are very high and their activities are often criticized in the mass media. When considering the advantages of collaborating with community groups to assist families, a child welfare government official cautioned, "It is the social worker who will be charged with criminal negligence, not the family resource program." The following section will look at some specific ways in which these differences have impact on the work of family resource programs.

Specific Issues

POWER IMBALANCE

The awesome mandate and legislative powers of the child welfare system can make interaction with its representatives intimidating for staff at family resource programs. A number of family resource practitioners described situations in which they were treated in ways that seemed to discount their knowledge and skills, their work, and their significance to a family. They report similar feelings of powerlessness to those of families.

> Going to a meeting at CAS is scary for me as an FRP staff person, and I'm not even the parent under surveillance.

> Even educated, professional staff become immobilized by the fear invoked by the myth (or reality) of child welfare.

> Some workers won't return calls, or they don't believe in what it is that you're trying to do with the families, or they don't even know what you're doing—and they don't want to know, because they have a very authoritarian view.

REPORTING ISSUES

Traditionally, for child welfare, "community involvement" meant "willingness to report." Family resource program staff do understand and accept their responsibility to report concerns for a child's safety to child welfare agencies, and many informants have in fact done so.

> We understand that child welfare workers are the experts in their field.

> It [reporting] was the right thing to do. It was the only thing to do.

Although most of the respondents to the questionnaire indicated that their programs had formal policies about reporting child abuse and neglect, many had none about related areas such as training requirements for staff and volunteers in recognizing and reporting child abuse and neglect, providing information to child welfare staff, and so on. Ensuring that adequate policies and procedures are in place and compatible with current legislation is very important. For example, policies that set out procedures such as waiting 24 hours before making a report or funnelling all concerns through senior staff, who in turn are responsible for making the report, may conflict with the requirements of the provincial or territorial legislation.

When making a report, many family resource program practitioners prefer to involve the parent or parents in the reporting process whenever possible. This differs from the process usually recommended by child welfare agencies, which is to make the report without alerting the family.

> Self-reporting is the ideal situation, because the family admits that they need help.

> When we fear for the immediate safety of the child, we ask the parent to phone the child welfare agency and we offer to go with the parent. We want the parent to feel empowered. We prefer that parents do not feel something is being done to them. We would make sure that the report is made.

Child welfare agencies may fear that consultation with parents before a report is made will result in a contamination of the investigation. Our informants were sensitive to this possibility also.

> My thoughts on that have changed. We used to have a policy that when we observed possible signs of child abuse, we would talk to the parents first before reporting. That was creating some difficulties. The investigation could be mud-

dled. We looked carefully at what we are here for. We are there for the parents but for the child first.

If a child discloses severe abuse, we would report directly to child welfare agencies. It is a matter of not muddying the water regarding the investigation.

For family resource programs, a major frustration occurs when there is a lack of appropriate action from child welfare agencies after a report has been made. A relationship of trust with a family may be seriously jeopardized in the process of making a report. If nothing happens as a result, the situation might well worsen since the family may withdraw and avoid further contact with the program. This means that the staff's ability to keep an eye on things and provide on-going assistance is lost. Practitioners feel that when they make a report, their judgement should carry more weight and go further to ensure action by child welfare agencies.

At times, child welfare had been notified and not intervened quickly or effectively to assist in a situation.

They ignored our recommendations and the child is still at risk.

The time lag between making the report and action being taken by the child welfare agency is very difficult for family resource program staff who are waiting "on pins and needles in the dark." Family resource programs frequently mentioned frustration about their inability to obtain information regarding the status of a case from child welfare agencies. Although they understand the ethical and regulatory basis for confidentiality, they feel that the reluctance to share even basic information indicates a lack of respect and understanding for their role as service providers.

I couldn't find out what happened to the family over the weekend, and I was worried sick.

Confidentiality very quickly becomes secrecy.

PUTTING TRUST-BASED RELATIONSHIPS AT RISK

Establishing positive relationships with families and communities is essential to the work of family resource programs. People come because they want to. Relationships built on mutual respect and trust develop slowly over time. Maintaining the hard-won yet sometimes fragile bond with a family is very important, especially when there may be a concern about child abuse or neglect, for in those circumstances, families need more than ever for someone to provide non-judgemental support and to help them access services. Yet embarrassment, anger, or fear may lead a family to isolate itself. Other families in the community may also decide to avoid the program as a consequence of involvement by child welfare.

> If a situation is reported and a police officer comes into the centre, the whole family is shamed. Many families lose trust with staff generally and it takes years to rebuild that trust. This is a real problem.

> It is better not to lose the trust of families under stress than to report too fast too soon.

> We have worked for months, or for years, to establish a relationship with this family and now they're connected and now they're here. The minute we report, then we wouldn't have that family back again … so what do we do?

PERCEIVED LACK OF SENSITIVITY AND UNDERSTANDING

In observing the work of child welfare agencies, many family resource program practitioners perceive a gap in child welfare workers' understanding of child development and attachment theory. Some believe that the child protection system misses the mark in both the short and long terms.

> The system does not seem to realize that it is abusing the child in ways the parent would never think of doing.

> Because of their lack of knowledge around child development, child welfare staff have unreasonable expectations and they often misinterpret things. For example, they need to learn how to interview children appropriately—not to put a young child across from them in a chair, but to get

down on the floor with the child and take enough time for the child to feel comfortable.

Usually the worker has no plans for important transitions such as saying goodbye. If this is not handled well, child and parent experience tremendous loss. It is rare that the parent is all bad, but there is virtually no preparation for the child and the parent. Kids will grow up to be parents, and these transitions are very important. They need compassion.

They had their own ideas about ensuring better outcomes for children.

Better to remove the abuser. Why remove the child? Removing a child from familiar surroundings puts him at greater risk. What's the message to the child who is punished for disclosing?

There should be a resource person inside the home to work with the entire family. Risk factors are compounded by being placed in care.

Reconstructing takes time and money. A few dollars spread over a longer period might work better than crisis dollars.

It is clear that many family resource practitioners believe that child welfare procedures add to children's distress unnecessarily. One comment reflected serious concerns: "I wonder whether the treatment is worse than the disease."

Unreasonable Expectations

Due to lack of awareness about each other's programs, inappropriate assumptions are sometimes made about what can reasonably be expected in the way of services and accountability. For example, some family resource programs reported that they felt pressured by child welfare agencies to provide a "quick fix" for parents who were being sent to attend their parenting courses. Although many would welcome more referrals by child welfare agencies, they wanted to be consulted. This negotiation, along with the parents' involvement, would demonstrate a collaborative approach and provide an opportunity for everyone to clarify expectations in advance, setting limits where necessary.

Respondents to the questionnaire reported that they did not always agree to requests from child welfare agencies. Some agreed to provide a service only if it was written in a plan-of-care agreement or court order. Others had refused requests because of concerns about liability, because the request was contrary to their family support role, or because they didn't have enough staff to provide the service. For family resource programs, the issue of providing services to parents who have been mandated by child welfare or the courts to attend programs is troubling.

> These are difficult situations. We are a voluntary service, and therefore if they've been mandated to accept our service, it usually doesn't work well.

> We are not in favour of taking references that are court driven, but it depends on the circumstances. We find that there is no learning and/or a lot of resistance to learning. If people don't want to be here, they have been very disruptive.

> I have agreed, but I have spent time (sometimes many hours) with the parents to shift the participation to voluntary rather than mandated.

> We are being requested to provide our service to mainly mandated parents. Currently, ourselves and similar organizations are working very hard to not have our services and participant groups defined by child protection. Some very real community development and parent/family support principles are at stake.

Given the formidable barriers that exist between family resource programs and child welfare agencies and the practical problems that arise as a result, we asked informants to share their ideas for improving working relationships. The suggestions in the next section include a number of strategies that are modest and informal and that lend themselves to implementation at the community level.

Reaching Out

INCREASED KNOWLEDGE AND UNDERSTANDING

Many family resource programs consulted during this investigation stated that they currently have positive relationships with child welfare. However, both child welfare staff and family resource program staff agreed that, in general, a better understanding of each other's work was called for in order to increase mutual respect and trust: "If they are going to refer clients to us, they must know our strengths and our limitations." One family resource centre was very pleased with the outcome of inviting a child welfare supervisor to sit on its board. While serving as a board member, the supervisor became aware of the centre's strengths. When she took that understanding back to her own workplace, the relationship between the two agencies noticeably improved.

LEARNING EACH OTHER'S NAMES

Family resource program staff frequently mentioned the enormous value of building personal relationships with individual staff members from the child welfare office. Although heavy case loads, busy schedules, and high turnover rates at child welfare agencies created many obstacles, informants agreed that the results of reaching out to connect were worth the effort.

Staff from both sectors consulted during this project suggested many ideas for getting to know their counterparts on a personal basis, such as dropping by each other's workplaces regularly; meeting informally at a monthly lunch open to all human service personnel in the community; working together on proposals and other community projects; providing presentations at each other's staff meetings; inviting child welfare staff to give workshops or training to parents, staff, and volunteers at the family resource program; participating in joint training activities; keeping each other informed about new programs; and working together to develop joint policies and protocols. Directors of family resource programs who had hired former child welfare workers were pleased with the new perspectives their programs had gained as a result.

ADDRESSING AND RESOLVING CONFLICTS

Addressing and resolving conflicts in a spirit of mutual respect can improve relationships.

> We work together on a community-based model of service delivery based on population health principles. Each success, conflict, or concern has contributed to stronger trust.

Some programs, such as those that were part of the Victoria project described in Chapter 3, have provided space in their centres for community workers from child welfare agencies, and these arrangements have been beneficial for everyone—the staff members of both organizations, the families, and the community.

CONSULTING ABOUT CONCERNS

Many family resource program informants mentioned that it would be very helpful, when there is concern about possible child abuse and neglect, if they could consult with a particular staff member at the child welfare agency before making a formal report. This contact person should understand and respect family support work and have enough seniority to be able to make discretionary decisions. The consultation would involve a discussion about the reasons for concern, whether the situation meets the threshold for reporting, what services are already in place to support the family, what action the child welfare agency is most likely to take after the report, and whether the parents should be encouraged to self-report. Some communities have established this type of consultation process, and it is generally working well.[4]

SUPPORTING FAMILIES THAT ARE CLIENTS OF CHILD WELFARE AGENCIES

Many family resource programs are already playing a significant role in supporting families that are involved with the child welfare system. While maintaining autonomy from child welfare services, they offer assistance and support to families in many ways, such as by providing referrals to community services like addiction counselling, anger management groups, family therapy, or family violence support groups. Frequently, they act as an advocate for the family or individual members by accompanying them to meetings and appointments, supplying background information to child welfare authorities, ensuring fair and respectful treatment, and gaining access to specialized services. Some programs offer respite child care for stressed families; some are willing to provide a location for visits with workers or with children in care. Occasionally, a family resource program has kept a child at its facility temporarily until an appropriate out-of-home placement can be found, so that the child can play in familiar surroundings rather than waiting at the child welfare office. Family resource programs should take a proactive approach in letting child welfare services know both the extent and the limitations of what they are able to offer families at all stages of their involvement with child welfare.

In the course of this project, we heard about many ways that families have been helped through the collaborative efforts of family resource programs and child welfare agencies. Two stories are shared here.

> Because of her past history, a young mother-to-be was informed by the child welfare agency that her baby would be taken into care immediately after birth. With the full co-operation of the child protection worker, a family support worker arranged a special time at the hospital to allow the mother to say goodbye to her baby. Through a quiet, tearful ritual that acknowledged the solemn importance of the occasion, the young woman was able to express her hopes and dreams for her baby's future and to let her baby go with dignity. This occasion, although certainly difficult for everyone involved, was important because the emotional needs of the mother were respected and she was able to exercise some control over the situation.

A different story of empowerment involves a mother of two very spirited preschoolers who had moved to a new community as a result of her husband's job.

> The mother was very isolated and lonely at home alone with the children and was not coping well. The children were taken into temporary care by the child welfare agency, and a condition for their return was that the mother not have the children in her sole care for more than four hours at a time. Although her husband could be home in the evenings, she was concerned about how she could meet this requirement during the day, so she contacted the family resource program co-ordinator for help. The co-ordinator organized a meeting with the child protection worker and two of the mother's neighbours who had offered help in the past. Together, they worked out a plan whereby the mother would volunteer at the centre every morning. Since the centre had a policy of providing child care for volunteers, the children could attend the preschool program at

the same time without fee. The two neighbours agreed to stop by the mother's home according to a pre-arranged schedule so that the four-hour limit would be respected during the rest of the day until the father got home. The child protection worker supported the plan, and the mother began an association with the centre that yielded many benefits. She had access to parenting resources, she learned new ideas from the preschool staff about directing her children's energy in positive ways, and she increased her self-esteem through her volunteer activities. In addition, she built an effective support network.

Conclusion

There is abundant evidence that family resource programs have much to offer families and, indeed, the child welfare enterprise itself. As this chapter has demonstrated, relationships between family resource programs and child welfare agencies are sometimes fraught with misunderstanding and distrust, and families are caught in the middle. Clearly, there is a pressing need to begin dialogue within and between these sectors in order to sort out better ways of working together in partnership with families. If honest and sincere, efforts to overcome long-standing differences at the community level will produce extraordinary results.

notes

1. This consultation involved 18 interviews (10 with staff from family resource programs, eight with child protection staff), the analysis of 70 written surveys received from family resource programs in each region, and the conduct of 18 focus groups in 11 communities (eight with staff from family resource programs, five with child protection staff, three with parents, one with government officials, and one with hospital-based social workers).

2. For further information about CAPC evaluations, contact National Program Officer, CAPC: (613) 952-7216. The evaluation of the first five years of the Better Beginnings, Better Futures projects in Ontario can be found at BBBF@queensu.ca.

3. Unless otherwise indicated, all quotes were gathered during the project from project interviews, focus groups, and questionnaires.

4. For an example of a protocol that sets out guidelines for a consultation
process, see *Child Abuse and Neglect Reporting Policies and Procedures: A Guide
for Toronto Family Resource Programmes*, published by the Metro Association
of Family Resource Programmes in 2000 and developed in consultation with
the Children's Aid Society of Toronto.

references

Ellis, D. 1998. *Finding Our Way: A Participatory Evaluation Method for Family
Resource Programs*. Ottawa: Canadian Association of Family Resource
Programs.

Globe and Mail. 2000. "Heroes Come in All Forms," 8 July.

Kellerman, M., and J. MacAulay. 1998. *Training and Professional Development in
the Family Resource Field*. Ottawa: Canadian Association of Family Resource
Programs.

Kyle, I., and M. Kellerman. 1998. *Case Studies of Canadian Family Resource
Programs: Supporting Families, Children and Communities*. Ottawa: Canadian
Association of Family Resource Programs.

Metro Association of Family Resource Programmes. 2000. *Child Abuse and
Neglect Reporting Policies and Procedures: A Guide for Toronto Family Resource
Programmes*. Toronto: author.

Schorr, L. 1997. *Common Purpose*. New York: Doubleday.

Sullivan, D. 1999. "Discovering Our Capacities," MSW project report,
Dalhousie University.

7

Building a Case for Community Approaches to Child Welfare

BRIAN WHARF

The final chapter identifies the lack of congruence between the mainstream approach to child welfare and community approaches. At the present time the mainstream approach is dominated by a paradigm of risk, and the values and assumptions of this paradigm are in many ways opposed to those that inform community approaches. The risk paradigm, while being justified on the grounds that it and its associated techniques protect children, also contains the considerable advantage of protecting policy-makers when instances of child neglect or abuse occur.

We began this book by asking why community approaches have remained on the periphery of practice. However, after reflecting on the case studies perhaps a more useful question is why these approaches have been tolerated at all! While community social work is the least threatening, the other community approaches outlined in the case studies represent a fundamental challenge to the status quo both at policy and practice levels. The case studies argue that the most hospitable auspices for community social work, particularly for community organization and community control, are agencies based in and responsible to the local community. While neighbourhood houses/family resource centres and First Nation agencies are the most conspicuous examples, other communities, like the Black community in Nova Scotia, also provide suitable auspices for community approaches.

Child Welfare as a Risk-focused Enterprise

The extent and dominance of the risk paradigm demand attention before we can proceed to build a case for community approaches. Many efforts have been made in recent years to improve policy and practice in child welfare, but these have been rooted in the concept of risk.

Houston and Griffiths (2000: 5) argue that "Risk has become an institutionalized and reified concept which dominates the thinking of policy-makers, managers and practitioners. Its ubiquity as a concept can be likened, in psychological terms, to a first-order construct—or a totalizing schema—against which other constructs such as client need are processed or rationed." Attempts to define and predict risk are not confined to child welfare, but have dominated practice in other fields of human service, such as corrections, policing, mental health, and community care for the elderly.

Douglas (1992: 27) points out risk assessment also "represents an attempt to investigate situations when things go wrong." And when things do go wrong the prevailing mood in society demands that someone be held accountable: a social worker for the death of a child, the parole board for releasing an offender who then commits a further crime, the surgeon who makes a mistake during an operation, or the nurse who fails to administer the proper medication. We concur with the following view from Australia.

> It is our contention that under the guise of protecting children, risk assessment instruments may essentially be devices designed to be used by bureaucratic, managerialist organizations in attempts to protect themselves from blame when tragedies occur. With risk assessment procedures in place, organizations are better placed to shift responsibility to individual workers when mistakes are made. (Goddard, et al., 1999: 258)

The demand for accountability has had the consequence of regulating, controlling, and inspecting practice. The simplest way of regulating practice is to put into effect standardized procedures like risk assessment instruments and to require that these be completed by individual workers with their respective clients. The introduction of computers into human service agencies allows managers to track whether workers correctly completed the forms and have followed up on the actions noted.

Risk assessment is firmly entrenched because it gives the impression to the media and the public that the safety of children will no longer be left to the unsupervised practice of individual social workers. Since all workers are required to apply the same instrument, judgements about neglect and abuse will be standardized across the agency.

We should add that prior to the ascendancy of the risk paradigm the dominant approach was casework, where those being served were viewed as "cases" and "clients." Like the risk paradigm, casework was based on the assumptions that the reason for becoming a client was the inability to deal with personal troubles and that these troubles could be dealt with by casework/counselling . The barriers to achieving these assumptions were large caseloads, which did not permit sufficient time for intensive counselling, and the lack of well-trained staff.

A Pathological View of Clients

The risk paradigm has had the consequence of introducing or rein-forcing the following characteristics of child welfare agencies. Risk assessments are focussed on the personal characteristics of parents and even more narrowly with identifying their deficits and weaknesses rather than their strengths and abilities. In its neglect of contextual social issues and networks of support, the risk paradigm presents a pathological view of those being served and reinforces an individualistic approach to prac-tice. Such a view confirms prevailing impressions in the media and even among some practitioners that individuals coming to the atten-tion of child welfare agencies are beset by personal problems like addic-tion, unstable relationships, and immaturity. While most live in poverty, in inadequate housing, and in unsafe neighbourhoods, the personal problems dominate and occupy the foreground while the public issues fade into the background.

An example will illustrate the point. In a research project my col-leagues and I were taken aback in a visit to a local ministry office in B.C. when in a discussion of the effects of poverty on child neglect and abuse, the child welfare staff responded that poverty was not a problem in their community (Callahan, Lumb, and Wharf, 1995). All agreed with the statement of one staff member who asserted that he had never taken a child into care because of poverty. At the request of the researchers the office administrator kept track of the income levels of the new clien-tele. After some months it was apparent that over 80 per cent were either receiving social assistance or were working at subsistence jobs for meagre pay. In subsequent discussions it became clear that since the vast major-ity of those being served were poor, staff had simply normalized this condition and had then identified personal problems as the reasons for the neglect and abuse of children.

This observation was confirmed in a later study in Ontario (Grant, 1998). Single parent clients of a Children's Aid Society reported that dealing with the lack of money was the most frustrating part of their lives. However, workers in the same agency focussed their attention on the ability of parents to look after their children. "It is interesting to see how the discourse implicitly accepts poverty as a reality in which child welfare workers work, as opposed to something they might do something about" (Grant, 1998: 41). The normalization of poverty by first-line workers is consistent with and reinforced by the policies and risk assessment procedures of their agencies.

Risk assessment instruments have also and appropriately been criticized for ignoring the substantial influences of gender, race, and culture. Indeed, Krane and Davies, two of the authors of the case studies in Montreal, extend this criticism by arguing that "the risk assessment trend has the potential to entrench oppressive relations of gender, race and class in child welfare practice with mothers" (Krane and Davies, 2000: 15).

A Crisis-ridden Environment

Crises and responding to crises have always been a feature of the child welfare enterprise, but in recent years this characteristic has been exacerbated by two complementary aspects of the risk paradigm, mandatory reporting and the requirement that all or at least the vast majority of complaints be investigated. The investigations are conducted in accordance with risk assessment instruments, which are detailed, comprehensive, and time-consuming. The consequence of these twin features is that many complaints are received and that the time and energy of staff are largely consumed by investigating them. Despite the fact that many complaints are ill-founded, if not downright frivolous or malicious, the focus on investigation creates a demanding workload and produces a mindset that effectively drives out interest in and time for alternative approaches. While complaints of large workloads and poor working conditions in child welfare are commonplace, it should also be noted that some child welfare staff thrive on the "commando" conditions that prevail; adrenalin rushes and the sense of importance that come from investigating complaints of neglect and abuse. Sometimes dangerous work can be exciting. The advertisement for staff noted in Chapter 6 quite clearly reveals that at least some child welfare agencies are looking for "commandos."

Politicized, Bureaucratized, and Hierarchical Organizations

For the most part child welfare agencies, whether cast in the form of departments of provincial governments or as Children's Aid Societies, are large, formal organizations. Policy-makers, whether politicians or senior managers, are usually middle-aged men who have little connection with or understanding of either the realities of the lives of first-line workers or those being served. The rules and regulations they create are often seen by first-line staff as silly or impractical or both and the contributions of line workers and clients are rarely considered.

As noted above, the cry for accountability demands that the work of staff be inspected and that standardized risk assessment instruments provide a most convenient way of conducting reviews. In turn, inspections require inspectors and in many jurisdictions the advent of risk assessments has resulted in adding staff to review the work of line staff and further steepening already hierarchical organizational structures.

In addition, when things go wrong, child welfare becomes a very public and politicized enterprise. The media launch into extensive coverage, highly divisive discussions occur in the provincial legislature, and the public—spurred on by the press—demands action and an end to child welfare tragedies.

Individual and Office-based Approaches to Practice

Individuals who come to the attention of child welfare agencies have traditionally been dealt with as individuals and interviews are conducted in the offices of child welfare workers. The risk paradigm reinforces this approach to practice. Some individuals prefer this arrangement since it seems to offer anonymity and assurance of confidentiality and replicates the practice of other professionals, such as lawyers and physicians. However, child welfare offices are often designed to "protect" staff from the occasional unruly client, and individuals desiring a middle-class office arrangement are quickly disillusioned by waiting rooms with shabby furniture, sturdy glass partitions separating receptionists from applicants, and restricted entry to the offices of staff. More importantly, this approach to practice does not allow those being served to get to know each other and to learn that many of the issues that surround them are shared by others.

In addition and with the exception of Quebec, provincial governments have not developed province-wide systems of community-based multi-service centres, assigning to these centres the responsibility of providing community-appropriate services. And, as revealed by the Montreal case study, some local community service centres or CLSCs have made a commitment to support neighbourhood or issue-based organizations that "try to maintain their autonomy and organize a program in which young mothers have a collective voice in defining their needs and shaping support programs" (see Chapter 3, Part II).

It is also clear from this case study that just as CLSCs encounter pressure from the Child and Youth Protection Centres to focus on families where children are at risk, grassroots organizations face the same demands from CLSCs. Resisting the pressure to "pathologize their clientele" requires that grassroots organizations develop a strong base of support from their constituents. Indeed, the interorganizational scene in Quebec is characterized by tension. While tension is often seen as disturbing and as a negative condition that should be eradicated, it is inevitable, given that provincial bureaucracies and grassroots organizations will often have conflicting objectives. Bureaucracies prize uniformity and standardization and these characteristics are inimical to the innovative and free-floating ways of community organizations. In our view it is infinitely more preferable to have community organizations and provincial departments engage in lengthy and tense negotiations than to have policies and programs in the human services decided at the provincial level without community input.

While many child welfare programs certainly can be seen as islands of excellence in all provinces, it is difficult to imagine any provincial government in Canada (with the possible exceptions of Manitoba and Quebec) implementing community approaches and implementing these as an integral part of practice. Manitoba is singled out because of its record of bringing about wide-scale reforms in child welfare and because of its announced intention to transfer responsibility for Métis and First Nations families living off reserve to the Manitoba Métis Federation and First Nations agencies (see Chapter 5. Part II). Quebec's comprehensive system of community-based services provides hospitable auspices for community approaches.

The Values and Assumptions of Community Approaches

As noted throughout this book, community approaches challenge the values and assumptions of the risk paradigm. Those being served are seen as citizens who are doing their best to care for and about their children in very stressful circumstances. Indeed, the public issues that pervade their lives would drive most middle-class professionals to distraction.

Community workers believe that the very fact that those being served can struggle against, and in many instances overcome, these adverse conditions is a clear indication that they have strengths. In turn, these strengths can be used not just for survival but for joining with others to overcome issues and to contribute to the life of the community. Community approaches, particularly those conceptualized by Rothman (1974) as community organizing, are most suitably located in neighbourhoods and in small and user-friendly agencies. At its best, community organizing assumes the responsibility of reporting on social conditions and advocating for change in policies that oppress people on the basis of colour, gender, race, and class.

Given the fundamental differences in values between risk and community paradigms, how have community approaches managed to gain even a toehold in child welfare? One way of coming to grips with this question is to conceptualize community approaches as innovative modes of practice that depart from and challenge the mainstream methods. An extensive literature has documented the difficulties of translating innovations into mainstream practice whether in child welfare or other fields of endeavour (see among many other sources, Rogers, 1962; Cameron and Vanderwoerd, 1999; and Schorr, 1988, 1997). Innovations are resisted precisely because they represent a challenge to the established ways of working and because in so doing they threaten those who are comfortable with, if not dedicated to, these established ways. And since the establishment is in control, innovators must find ways to surmount resistance. Innovations often fade away against such steep resistance, but this has not occurred in the case of community approaches.

One reason for the toehold is that the first-line workers and their supervisors who were committed to a community approach championed it within their agency and had the courage and tenacity to pursue it. They were innovators whose legitimacy and standing in their agencies enabled them to propose and to support community approaches. Some of the early proponents deserve particular mention. In the Toronto Children's Aid Society, the original group of community workers included Audrey McLaughlin, who later became MP for Yukon and leader of the New Democratic Party, and Doug Barr, whose subsequent career included work as Executive Director of the Canadian Cancer Society and of Goodwill Industries of Los Angeles. As noted in Chapter 3, Part I, Riley Hern is well known throughout the B.C. Ministry for Children and Families as a respected and innovative practitioner.

A second reason is that these champions received support in their agencies. Unless champions are senior staff with the authority to initiate and implement change by ensuring that resources will be made available, they cannot launch innovations on their own. While full and unequivocal support for community approaches has never been forthcoming, most of the initiatives reported in the case studies have enjoyed some support from senior staff. Thus, the regional manager of the Ministry for Children and Families who is responsible for all child welfare services in Victoria reported to the writer that "if the neighbourhood houses are prepared for the protection of children I think it is ideal for our staff to have a regular presence in and be available to the community" (Cowell, 2000: 1). The Executive Director of the Toronto Children's Aid Society is unequivocal in his support for the community program. "We feel that this is a remarkable program. Its staff have been able to mobilize communities to take responsible action for their children and to organize around critical social issues such as child poverty, a lack of affordable housing and inadequate child care resources" (Rivers, in Chapter 4, Part II).

Third, community approaches have worked in rural offices of provincial ministries of welfare. The relative isolation of these offices frees them from the direct gaze of head office, and the combination of location and of social work staff members committed to an innovation has provided a unique opportunity to tailor practice to the needs of community. Such has been the case in Hazelton where Maurice Yee, Greg Kormany, and Tanya Buttress have developed a community social work approach by being sensitive to the culture and traditions of the community in which they work.

Despite their tireless work, most of the champions of community approaches are first-line staff and supervisors like Riley Hern and Sharron Richards and their time and energy are devoted to preserving their fragile community programs. Hence, it is not surprising that they have been unable to convince provincial politicians that community approaches are an effective way of protecting children. Community approaches are often viewed as "mucking about" in the community, a set of disorganized efforts ranging from criticizing the inadequacy of provincial policies (and thereby treading on the toes of politicians) to organizing self-help discussion groups that seem to have little connection to the care and protection of children. On the other hand, the risk paradigm promises clarity and control and may well dominate the child welfare enterprise for the foreseeable future. Nevertheless, our commitment to community approaches is such that we explore all possible ways of incorporating them into child welfare.

Building a Case for Community Approaches

PRYING OPEN THE POLICY WINDOW

If a community paradigm is to be adopted it will be implemented through legislation and policy statements. A useful framework for considering how policy changes occur is the concept of the policy window. Kingdon (1995) argues that substantial changes in policy occur when three ingredients combine to open the policy window. These ingredients are a problem or focussing event, a political environment that is favourable to change, and policy specialists who can suggest remedies or solutions to the problem. The introduction of risk assessment instruments provides an apt illustration of the persuasive power of the framework: a focussing event has often been the death of or serious injury to a child; the media and public have provided a sympathetic environment by urging that substantial changes are required, and policy specialists have emerged to advance the risk paradigm.

Our case begins by asserting that there is a problem that extends beyond the focussing event of an individual tragedy. The problem is that the child welfare enterprise is in such disarray that it may be close to collapse. Consider the following from Hart (2001: 17):

> Fifty per cent of the child welfare consultants in New Brunswick are retiring. Prince Edward Island social workers consider child and family services in crisis. Saskatchewan social workers staged a provincial day of protest. There are calls for reform to the Alberta child welfare system. Yellowknife social workers have filed a grievance citing dangerous conditions because of high caseloads. Newfoundland/Labrador echoes workload concerns. Nova Scotia is concerned about training and service coordination issues.

And yet another review of child welfare has been conducted in B.C. because of workload issues in the northern region of the province.

Should these examples of systemic failure continue, the risk paradigm may no longer be sustainable. Paradigms hold sway only as long as they are seen to be effective, and the perception of effectiveness is often persuasive in a field such as child welfare, where empirical evidence is rarely available. Hence, the collapse or even sustained questioning of the risk paradigm might create the second ingredient for change, an environment in which proponents could advance the case for a community paradigm.

Policy specialists are the third ingredient required to open the policy window. According to Kingdon, policy specialists can be found both within and external to the state and it is in the external community that policy specialists will be found to push for community approaches. Indeed, the label of "policy specialists" is unfortunate since it conjures up images of powerful civil servants and influential consulting firms. Such individuals are not likely to be supporters of community approaches. Rather, the policy specialists for community approaches will emerge from the ranks of first line-workers, supervisors, those being served, and the staff of neighbourhood houses and First Nations agencies. Band and tribal council chiefs and agency directors are uniquely placed to argue the case for culturally appropriate and community-controlled services. In addition, academics who have articulated the potential of community approaches would be useful allies in proposing the case for change (see, for example, Lee and Richards in this volume; Adams and Nelson, 1995; Hudson 1999; Smale, 1995; Wharf, 1997).

The case would be more powerfully made if this disparate group could unite in a campaign for community approaches. And while we would applaud a national organizing effort by a consortium of agencies such as the Canadian Council on Social Development, the Vanier Institute for the Family, the National Poverty Association, and the Child Welfare League of Canada, we recognize that such an ambitious effort may well be beyond the resources and the mandate of these agencies. Rather, we think the case will be made slowly, by the differences that will emerge between the community approaches of neighbourhood houses and First Nations agencies on the one hand and the risk-dominated and intrusive approach of mainstream child welfare organizations on the other.

As Chapter 6 points out, family resource centres and neighbourhood houses are designed to serve all children and families and not just those experiencing problems. Because of this philosophy and the programs they offer, they have the potential to become the backbone of the community service sector. These centres could become the home of preventive services and at least theoretically they provide hospitable auspices for all community approaches. However, the record to date indicates that many centres have yet to vigorously pursue community organizing activities that border on social reform, perhaps because of an unwillingness to annoy the state and to jeopardize funding.

Should the family resource centres movement prosper and illustrate the potential of community approaches, the formal child welfare enterprise might realize the benefits to be gained, and adopt the community paradigm. Is it too optimistic to expect that by working in close touch with community resource centres, formal child welfare agencies will be persuaded of the efficacy of community approaches or at least of community social work—a case of positive contamination?

Despite our enthusiasm for neighbourhood houses and family resource centres we are reluctant to assign the mandate for prevention solely to them, leaving the formal child welfare enterprise mired in an investigative mode. The experience in the Victoria project clearly reveals the limitations of this division of labour. When investigations are carried out without the benefit of a relationship with the family they are often intrusive and result in alienating families from seeking help in times of stress. Intrusive investigations can damage the positive relationships established between residents and staff of neighbourhood houses.

In addition, complaints that children are being neglected or abused are made in an anonymous fashion. While the intent behind anonymity is to encourage professionals and citizens to report all of the instances of neglect and abuse that come to their attention, the downside is that neighbours or former partners can launch ill-founded or even malicious reports. The experience of some parents is that community can take the form of neighbours acting as watchdogs rather than as helpers. One mother interviewed for a research project provided a telling example of this point. When living in an apartment with her active and noisy boys, her fellow residents reported their suspicions of neglect and abuse to the ministry. When she moved into a house the complaints ceased despite the fact that her sons remained as rambunctious as ever (Weller and Wharf, 1996).

INCORPORATING COMMUNITY SOCIAL WORK INTO PRESENT PRACTICE

As noted earlier, community social work does not constitute a major threat to mainstream policy and practice and could transform intrusive investigations into offers of help and assistance. The experiences of the Victoria project and Hazelton office illustrate the potential of community social work and it has been successfully introduced in the U.K. and in some jurisdictions in the U.S. (Adams and Nelson, 1995). These precedents can provide some support and comfort to agencies in Canada that decide to introduce community social work as the basis of practice.

Support for the concept of community social work comes from some critiques of the risk paradigm. It will be recalled from Chapter 1 and from the case studies of Hazelton and the Victoria project that community social work is all about engaging with people to work through their troubles in a collaborative fashion. Community social work draws on and contributes to the resources of the community in dealing with problems. In much the same vein Houston and Griffiths (2000: 8) argue that changing the risk paradigm will require that "professionals be dethroned of their expert status and participate alongside parents, children and significant others to attain a reasoned and fair decision."

While acknowledging the difficulties in altering the risk paradigm, Houston and Griffith derive some comfort from Handy's analysis of organizational development (Handy, 1985). Handy identifies three phases of organizational development: pioneer, scientific, and integrated. Initiation and early growth characterize the pioneer phase, centralization and bureaucratization represent the scientific phase, and the integrative phase is a "more adaptable, innovative customer driven culture. In focusing on the customer, the professional style becomes participative and democratic" (Houston and Griffith. 2000: 8). Family group conferences where all involved participated in reaching a plan for a family provide an example of the participative style of working, but after a promising introduction in Newfoundland these conferences have not been implemented in other provinces. (For discussion of the Newfoundland experiences with family group conferences, see Burford and Pennell, 1995).

While the argument that child welfare organizations will attain the integrative phase is appealing, we recognize that the customer in child welfare is typically a person of low status and beset by a host of difficulties. Such customers are too busy and have insufficient influence to push child welfare agencies into adopting a participative style of management and introducing community social work.

Perhaps the most important source of change will come from First Nations tribal and band councils. As the case studies in Chapter 6 illustrate, child welfare agencies in First Nations communities are carving out approaches based on tradition and culture and take a holistic approach in considering both personal troubles and public issues. These agencies serve all families and not just those with problems—they invite all members of the community to engage in planning new programs that are suited to the community. In addition, First Nations agencies are convinced of the need to build environments that support families and children and they have confronted provincial ministries when provincial legislation and policy run counter to their objectives.

Indeed, some First Nations agencies are leading the way in child welfare. These agencies have demonstrated that they can take a community social work approach to both the support and investigative functions and can engage in community organizing to change negative environments. As First Nations agencies become more numerous and as the benefits of their approach become more evident, the mainstream child welfare enterprise may well find it difficult to continue its intrusive mode of practice. We note again the reminder in Chapter 1 that while First Nations agencies should not be subject to the kind of irritating and unhelpful regulations cited in the Lalum'utul Smun'eem case study, First Nations must develop their unique national or provincial standards to ensure that "acute localitis" (Montgomery,1979) does not develop.

Comparisons between the mainstream approach and that of neighbourhood houses and First Nations agencies will be aided if the latter can provide evidence of their effectiveness. The mainstream approach has never been examined through rigorous and ongoing research to investigate its record of success in protecting children. Indeed, as pointed out repeatedly in this book, the combined experience of those being served and of child welfare staff argues that it is not effective. Yet, in order to convince politicians and their senior advisers to bring community approaches into the mainstream of agency practice, these new approaches must provide evidence of effectiveness—an irony of no small proportion!

We acknowledge that the evidence of effectiveness of community approaches is as yet far from conclusive. To our knowledge there have been only a few attempts in Canada to establish careful comparative studies where these approaches have been established in some but not in other communities. Two studies of mutual aid and support networks were noted in Chapter 1, and both concluded that these programs had been effective (Cameron, 1995; Fuchs, 1995). For the most part we are left looking for proximate measures of effectiveness, but despite the best efforts of the authors of the case studies to identify measures only a few were found.

One indicator was noted in Chapter 3, Part 1: tracking the way in which children come into care. In the past five years 125 children have come into the care of the Hazelton office and in only two instances did parents contest the decision. Other indicators relate to the reduction in social problems. The authors of the Cowichan case study report in Chapter 5, Part 1 that "the Cowichan community is much healthier that it was a decade ago. Before Lalum'utul'Smun'eem began, alcohol abuse and family violence were community norms. Today, while these continue to be a problem for some families, they are the exception rather than the norm." In Chapter 4, Part 1, McKenzie notes that the community work program of the Winnipeg Child and Family Service agency was responsible for a sharp decline in the number of complaints of child neglect in one inner city area. And the West Region Child and Family Services was awarded the Peter T. Drucker Award for Canadian Non-Profit Innovation for its use of block funding and the medicine wheel framework in developing its services and programs.

The case study of the Children's Aid Society of Toronto (Chapter 4, Part II) provides many concrete examples of community program outcomes in that agency. Community workers have assisted residents to develop programs that meet the particular needs of their neighbourhoods and in so doing have increased their confidence and ability to bring about change and created useful resources.

An important contribution to the changes recommended here could come from schools of social work. As a number of commentators have observed, community organizing as a field of study has virtually disappeared from curricula (Lee and Richards, Chapter 4, Part II; Callahan and Wharf, 1999) and until recently insufficient attention was given to child welfare. However, a number of schools have entered into partnerships with provincial ministries of child welfare to develop curricula on child welfare (Armitage, Callahan, and Lewis, 2001). Schools could provide some badly-needed leadership by making the community social work approach the bedrock of this new venture in child welfare. In addition, reviving courses on community organization and co-operating with First Nations agencies in their efforts to develop culturally sensitive programs would be a most valuable contribution.

It is crucial that the leaders in child welfare, be they First Nations agencies, neighbourhood houses, or child welfare agencies, take on the responsibility of reporting on social conditions on a regular basis. They are in a pivotal position to report on the circumstances of those being served and in so doing alter the image from bad mother and ungrateful welfare recipient to one of a harassed individual doing the best she or he can to survive in very difficult circumstances. Failure to embrace social reporting reinforces the position that there are no public issues, merely private troubles. And a national organization like the Child Welfare League of Canada or the National Council on Welfare might then take on the task of aggregating local and provincial reports into a national profile.

To conclude, the case studies provide examples of effective practice. Community social work in Hazelton and the Victoria project demonstrate that it is possible to treat those being served in a respectful fashion, to involve them in making plans, and to assist them to overcome the enormous difficulty of raising children in poverty. The work of the Toronto Children's Aid Society and the Winnipeg Child and Family Services illustrates that community organizing efforts alter environments, develop new programs and build community capacity. The West Region Family Services and the Lalum'utul' Smun'eem agencies have gained control of child welfare and have incorporated community social work and community organizing with cultural traditions of child care.

In responding to the question posed at the beginning of the book, whether community approaches can be brought into the mainstream, we identified the dissonance between the two approaches and the values that underpin them. Given the extent of the dissonance, the first response to the question was to rephrase it and ask why community approaches have been allowed to exist even on the margin. The answer seems to lie in the tireless work of first line workers and supervisors in mainstream agencies.

If community approaches are to move into the mainstream, a shift in paradigms will be required: from the risk paradigm that dominates child welfare at the present time to a community paradigm that would be based on the approaches of community social work, community organizing, and community control. And we reiterate that community approaches are necessary, but not sufficient. Without a commitment to progressive social policies such as those enunciated in chapter one, community approaches will not achieve their full potential.

In view of its attraction to senior policy-makers, we do not see the risk paradigm as being in imminent danger of collapse. But we are of the view that risk is basically a flawed paradigm. It treats line staff as technicians and those being served as objects and will ultimately fail and be replaced. At that point, some policy specialists will be required to make the case for a community paradigm that protects children by involving parents and "eyes on the street." A consortium of those being served, line workers, staff of First Nations agencies, and community-oriented academics would be an ideal group to lead the way.

references

Adams, P., and K. Nelson, eds. 1995. *Reinventing Human Services, Community and Family Centered Practice.* New York: Aldine de Gruyter.

Armitage, A., M. Callahan, and C. Lewis. (Forthcoming). "Social Work Education and Child Protection: The B.C. Experience," *Canadian Social Work Review.*

Burford, G. and J. Pennel. 1995. "Family Group Decision Making: An Innovation in Child and Family Welfare," in J. Hudson and B. Galaway, eds., *Child Welfare in Canada: Research and Policy Implications.* Toronto: Thompson Educational Publishing.

Callahan, M., C. Lumb, and B. Wharf. 1995. *Protecting Children by Empowering Women.* Victoria: University of Victoria, School of Social Work, Family and Community Research Program.

Callahan, M., and B. Wharf. 1999. "Reclaiming Community Organizing in Social Work," *Perspectives: Newsletter of the B.C. Association of Social Workers* 21,3: 10-11.

Cameron, G. 1995. "The Nature and Effectiveness of Parent Mutual Aid Organizations in Child Welfare," in J. Hudson and B. Galaway, eds., *Child Welfare in Canada: Research and Policy Implications.* Toronto: Thompson Educational Publishing.

Cameron, G., and J. Vanderwoerd. 1997. *Protecting Children and Supporting Families: Promising Programs and Organizational Realities.* New York: Aldine de Gruyter.

Cowell, J. 2000. Personal communication with B. Wharf.

Douglas, M. 1992. *Risk and Blame: Essays in Cultural Theory.* London: Routledge and Kegan Paul.

Fuchs, D. 1999. "Preserving and Strengthening Families and Protecting Children: Social Network Intervention, A Balanced Approach to the Prevention of Child Maltreatment," in J. Hudson and B. Galaway, eds., *Child Welfare in Canada: Research and Policy Implications.* Toronto: Thompson Educational Publishing.

Goddard, C.R., B.J. Saunders, J.R. Stanley, and J. Tucci. 1999. "Structured Risk Assessment Procedures: Instruments of Abuse?" *Child Abuse Review* 8: 251-63.

Grant, L. 1998. "Moving from Punishment and Treatment to Empowerment in Child Welfare Practice: Is It Possible?," York University, School of Social Work.

Handy, C. 1985. *Understanding Organizations.* London: Penguin Books.

Hart, R. 2001. "The National Report," *Perspectives: Newsletter of the B.C. Association of Social Workers* 23,1: 17.

Houston, S., and H. Griffiths. 2000. "Reflections on Risk in Child Protection: Is It Time for a Shift in Paradigms?," *Child and Family Social Work* 5: 1-10.

Hudson, P. 1999. "Community Development and Child Protection: A Case for Integration," *Community Development Journal* 34,4: 346-56.

Kingdon, J.K. 1995. *Agendas, Alternatives and Public Policies.* New York: Harper and Row.

Krane, J., and L. Davies. 2000. "Mothering and Child Protection Practice: Rethinking Risk Assessment," *Child and Family Social Work* 5: 35-45.

Montgomery, J. 1979. "The Populist Front in Rural Development: Or Shall We Eliminate the Bureaucrats and Get On With The Job?," *Public Administration Review* (Jan.-Feb.): 58-65.

Rivers, B. 2000. Personal communication to B. Lee and S. Richards.

Rogers, E. 1962. *Diffusion of Innovation.* New York: Free Press.

Rothman, J. 1974. "Three Models of Community Organization Practice," in J. Cox, J. Tropman, J. Ehrlich, and J. Rothman, *Strategies of Community Organization.* Itasca, IL.: Peacock Press.

Schorr, L.B. 1988. *Within Our Reach: Breaking the Cycle of Disadvantage.* New York: Anchor Books.

———. 1997. *Common Purpose: Strengthening Families and Neighbourhoods to Rebuild America.* New York: Anchor Books.

Smale, G. 1995. "Integrating Community and Individual Practice: A New Paradigm for Practice," in P. Adams and K. Nelson, eds., *Reinventing Human Services, Community and Family Centered Practice.* New York: Aldine de Gruyter, 59-86.

Weller, F. and B. Wharf. 1996. "From Risk Assessment to Family Action Planning," University of Victoria. School of Social Work.

Wharf, B. 1997. "Reframing Child Welfare," *Canada's Children* 4,1: 11-17.

White, D. 1994. "The Community Management of Exclusion," *Lien social et politiques—RIAQ* 32: 37-51.

contributors

CANDACE BERNARD ☛ is a social worker with the children-in-care team of the Department of Community Services in Dartmouth, Nova Scotia. She holds Master's degrees in social work and education and has a particular interest in the intersection of schooling and social justice issues and their impact on marginalized populations. Ms. Bernard is a part-time employee of the Nova Scotia Association of Black Social Workers.

WANDA BERNARD ☛ is Associate Professor and Director, Maritime School of Social Work, Dalhousie University. She teaches anti-oppressive and direct social work practice. Her research interests are critical race theory, Africentricity, and participatory action research. Dr. Bernard is a founding member of the Nova Scotia Association of Black Social Workers.

LESLIE BROWN ☛ is Associate Professor and Director, School of Social Work, University of Victoria, and an instructor in the Master's program in Indigenous Government. Dr. Brown's scholarly and practice interests include Aboriginal governance issues and anti-oppressive social work practice.

LINDA DAVIES ☛ is Assistant Professor, School of Social Work, McGill University and teaches in the areas of child welfare, the social construction of mothering, and qualitative research methods. Dr. Davies is the co-editor of and a contributor to *Bureaucracy and Community* (1990) and is currently involved in research inquiring into practice in feminist organizations.

KAREN FOX ☛ is a social worker with Batshaw Youth and Family Centres, a youth protection agency in Montreal. She is a graduate student at the School of Social Work, McGill University. Her current research interests are exploring women's relationships to child welfare practice.

LISA HADDOCK ➤ is the Executive Director of Lalum'utul' Smun'eem Child and Family Services. Lisa earned her BSW from the University of Victoria and her practice is focussed on community development in First Nations communities. She has worked in child welfare for more than eight years, is the mother of a three-year-old boy, and takes an active interest in First Nations child welfare issues at the provincial and national levels.

BILL LEE ➤ has been a community organizer and teacher for over 25 years. He is Associate Professor at the School of Social Work, McMaster University. He has been engaged in child welfare, First Nations development, international social development, and housing co-operatives. Dr. Lee is the author of *Pragmatics of Community Organization* (1999) and, with Mike Balkwill, *Participatory Planning for Action* (1996).

MARGARET KOVACH ➤ is Saulteaux from southern Saskatchewan and holds a Master of Social Work degree from Carleton University. She has worked with several First Nations communities in B.C. as a community therapist, sexual abuse counsellor, and supervisor of a First Nations family support program. She is currently a sessional instructor for the School of Social Work, University of Victoria, and the co-ordinator of the Aboriginal Social Work Training Program.

JULIA KRANE ➤ is an Assistant Professor in the School of Social Work at McGill University. Her scholarly interests centre on violence against women and children with particular emphasis on front-line intervention in such settings as youth protection agencies and battered women's shelters. Dr. Krane's research is guided by feminist theory.

JANICE MACAULAY ➤ is a Certified Family Educator and has extensive experience in parenting education and family support. After working for 10 years at an Ottawa family resource program, she joined the Canadian Association of Family Resource Programs as a researcher. She is now the Co-ordinator, Information and Project Development, and co-ordinates Nobody's Perfect, a program for parents of young children.

BRAD MCKENZIE ➤ is Professor in the Faculty of Social Work, University of Manitoba. He has completed a number of research studies in child welfare, particularly in First Nations child and family services. Dr. McKenzie was co-editor of *Canadian Social Work Review* from 1986 to 1998 and is the co-author of *Connecting Policy to Practice in the Human Services* (1998).

SHARRON RICHARDS ➤ has worked
in child welfare for the past 30 years.
While her experience included intake
and family service, for the past 26
years she has been engaged in rural
and urban community development
with the Children's Aid Societies of
Toronto and York Region. Currently
she is the manager of the community
development and prevention program
and the child welfare advocate at the
Children's Aid Society of Toronto.

ERIC SHRAGGE ➤ is Associate Professor
in the School of Community and Public
Affairs, Concordia University. He is
the director of the Graduate Diploma
Program in Community Economic
Development. Dr. Shragge has written
on community organization and social
policy and is the co-editor of *Bureaucracy
and Community* (1990) and of *Social
Economy-International Debates and
Perspectives* (2000).

VERONICA STRONG-BOAG ➤ is a historian
working in Educational Studies and
Women's Studies at the University of
British Columbia. A former president
of the Canadian Historical Association,
she has published extensively on the
history of Canadian women and children. Dr. Strong-Boag's books include
*The New Day Recalled. Lives of Girls
and Women in English Canada, 1919-
1939* (1998); *Rethinking Canada: The
Promise of Women's History* (1992, 1997,
1998, and 2001); *British Columbia Re-
considered, Essays on Women* (1991);

*Paddling Her Own Canoe: The Times
and Texts of E. Pauline Johnson
(Tekahionwake) 1861-1913* (2000).

BRIAN WHARF ➤ is Professor Emeritus,
School of Social Work and Faculty
of Human and Social Development,
University of Victoria. During his
years at this university he was Director,
School of Social Work; Dean, Faculty
of Human and Social Development;
Professor and graduate adviser in a
policy/practice program; and Acting
Director, School of Public Administration. Dr. Wharf's most recent book,
co-authored with Brad McKenzie, is
Connecting Policy and Practice (1998).

index

drop-in, 71
publicly funded, 44
death of a child, 48, 85, 137, 189
accountability, 182
deficit approach, 143, 166–67
delegation, 136, 140, 145–46, 150
Delegation Enabling Agreement,
136–37
Department of Indian and Northern
Affairs (INAC), 136
drug abuse. *See* substance abuse
Duplessis orphans, 43

early intervention. *See* intervention,
early
East End Young Moms Project, 105
education, 40, 100
charter schools, 42
compulsory schooling, 36, 40
humanizing schooling, 36
inclusive schooling, 44
Prince Albert Indian Residential
School, 43
public, 40
Residential School Project, 134
residential schools, 36, 40, 42–43,
142
special needs schools, 42
universal, 39–40
effectiveness, 55–57
assessing, 87
of community approaches, 193
elders, 134, 145, 153
impact of professionalization,
140–41
self-conscious traditionalism, 149
teachings, 132
Equally Healthy Kids, 105
extended families, 58, 132, 158
Cowichan people, 149–50
kinship system, 153
support, 143, 145

Factories, Shops, and Mine Acts, 36
family breakdown, 96
family centres, 18, 74

family conferences, 52, 60, 192
family resource programs, 10, 19, 21,
24, 165, 181, 190–91. *See also*
community resource centres;
neighbourhood houses
authority, 166
child development knowledge,
173–74
collaborative efforts with child welfare, 178
dialogues with child welfare services, 163, 177, 179
effectiveness, 164
and family strengths, 167
funding, 88
locality development, 20, 98
mandate, 166
personal relationships with child
welfare staff, 176
reporting child abuse, 170–72
requests from child welfare, 175
settings, 169
trust, 173
work environments, 168
FAS/E. *See* fetal alcohol syndrome and
effects
feminists, 29, 32, 36, 38, 78. *See also*
women
analysts, 63
on education, 41
on risk assessment, 54
writers, 12
fetal alcohol syndrome and effects,
155–56
First Nation(s), 10, 12–13, 23, 30, 50,
91, 131–62
Aboriginal caregivers, 158
Aboriginal resistance, 36
child sexual abuse disclosures, 135
community organization, 152
community-oriented approach, 160
Cowichan values and beliefs,
132–34, 149–50
cultural context, 147
culturally appropriate services, 24,
155, 158, 161, 190, 194